The
NATURALIST'S
GARDEN

Published by Ebury Press
Division of the National Magazine Company Ltd,
Colquhoun House, 27-37 Broadwick Street, London W1V 1FR

ISBN 0 85223 661 1

This book was devised and produced by Templar Publishing Ltd,
107 High Street, Dorking, Surrey RH4 1QA

Editor: Moyna Kitchin
House editor: Beatrice Phillpotts
Designer: Mike Jolley
Typesetting: Templar Type

Colour separations, printing and binding by Motta, Milan, Italy.

The NATURALIST'S GARDEN

JOHN FELTWELL

EÐ

EBURY
PRESS

ACKNOWLEDGEMENTS

The photographs in this book are reproduced by kind permission of the following:

ARCAID/Richard Bryant, 93; Ashmolean Museum, Oxford, 69 (*right*), 70; John Bethell, 44/45, 48, 64/65, 82/83, 85 (*top*), 132 (*top*), 133 (*top*); Bibliothèque Nationale, Paris, 30/31; Biofotos, 139 (*top*), 157; Bodleian Library, 17 (*Douce 310*), 80 (Rawlinson Copperplate 29); The Bridgeman Art Library, 59 (*top*); British Library, 28, 57, 68, 77 (*top*), 79, 102 (*bottom*); June Chatfield, The Gilbert White Museum, Selborne, 88; Country Life Magazine, 123 (*top*); E.T. Archive, 40, 43 (*left*), 73, 75, 86, 91 (*bottom*), 96, 99, 106/107, 114 (*top*), 117; Mary Evans Picture Library, 42, 74, 91 (*top right*), 104 (*top*), 105 (*top*), 111 (*right*), 112, 116 (*top*), 119 (*right*); John Feltwell/Wildlife Matters, 12, 16, 19, 22, 23, 24, 26, 33 (*right*), 34, 35 (*right*), 36, 37, 47, 51, 52, 54/55, 58, 59 (*bottom*), 71, 72, 77 (*bottom*), 78, 87 (*bottom*), 90, 91 (*top left*), 92, 94, 101 (*top*), 103, 105 (*bottom*), 110, 114 (*bottom*), 116 (*bottom*), 118, 120, 124, 130 (*bottom*), 132 (*bottom*), 133 (*bottom*), 134, 136, 138, 140 (*left*), 141, 145, 146, 148, 149, 151 (*right*), 153, 155, 156; Fine Art Photographic Ltd, 20; Gallery Five, 128; Robert Harding, 125 (*top*); Jerry Harpur, 6, 39, 100, 101 (*bottom*); Impact Photos/Pamla Toler, 119 (*left*), 135; The MacQuitty International Photographic Collection, 22/23, 60, 98, 111 (*left*); Mansell Collection, 14/15, 53; P. Morris/Wildlife Matters, 89, 152, 154; Tony Mott, 18, 33 (*left*), 35 (*left*), 49, 67, 109; The National Gallery, 54; National Portrait Gallery, 85 (*bottom*), 122; National Postal Museum, 139 (*bottom*); New-York Historical Society, 125 (*bottom*); NHPA, 8; Royal Botanic Garden, Edinburgh, 140 (*rightr*); © Scala/Firenze, 10/11; Städelsches Kunstinstitut, Frankfurt am Main, 27; Stiftsbibliothek St Gallen, 25; Tony Stone, 105 (*top*); Sutton Place Foundation, 126/127, 137; Uppsala Universitet, 87 (*top*); Vision International, 104 (*bottom*); Walters Art Gallery, Baltimore, 38; Weidenfeld & Nicolson Ltd, 43 (*right*) and 50/John Freeman, 69 (*left*)/Clive Boursnell, 76/John Freeman, 129/Tony Evans, 130 (*top*)/Jane Bown, 129, 142/143 & 151 (*left*)/Clay Perry; Whittet Books Ltd, 13, 15; Windsor Castle, Royal Library. Her Majesty The Queen, 97; George Wright, 130/131.

CONTENTS

*Planting a "wild" lawn will help to
conserve the plant and insect variety
of our vanishing traditional
meadows.*

FOREWORD

The history of gardening is primarily about taming plants from the wild to please us, the gardeners, in one way or another – for shade, coolness and beauty, as well as food, medicine and other useful attributes

Most of our herbs, in particular, are straight from the wild, and among the earliest to be deliberately grown, for their medicinal properties (real or imagined) and their culinary ones. The earliest books are herbals and only gradually does appreciation of beauty and curiousness in plants appear. In our own relatively delayed civilization (compared with Chinese, Egyptian and Roman) there is, for instance, a kind of quantum leap in this respect between Gerard's *Herball* of 1597 and Parkinson's *Paradisi in Sole, Paradisus Terrestris . . .* of 1629.

Although many of our ornamental plants have been much altered by selection and breeding, we still grow a large number of true species, and the inquisitive can research their origins and how they reached our gardens to create there a remarkable community of nations. This is a valid aspect of natural history, and so is a study of the weeds among the ornamentals, plague though they may be. One may curse the deep-spreading roots of bindweed or horsetail, the tubers of celandine, the quick-maturing seeds of thistle, chickweed and groundsel; but weeds are such well-designed opportunists that they are among the marvels of nature.

Apart from its plants, the most ordinary garden abounds in creatures. There will certainly be birds and insects, probably hedgehogs, squirrels, newts and frogs. But beyond the birds, few people think of their gardens at all as haunts of wildlife, though they react more or less strongly to the usually unwanted creatures gardening particularly encourages – aphids, whiteflies, caterpillars, weevils, slugs and snails, woodlice, mildews and rusts; it sounds like the seven plagues of Egypt. The average gardener's attention to organisms like these is effectively a study of natural history, even if extirpation is the aim.

John Feltwell takes a dispassionate view of such populations, showing us for instance what an average tree can harbour. His sketch of garden history from earliest times is slanted at all points towards those who realised that gardens reflect and absorb nature however formalized they may be; gardeners from Pliny to Jefferson; writers like Shakespeare, who certainly knew his flowers and what they meant to ordinary people; collectors who observed aspects of nature beyond the plants they specifically sought; naturalists who used their own gardens for observation, like Fabre and Darwin; gardeners who wished to encourage wildlife like Winston Churchill.

Today there is a strong trend towards more "wild gardening", to encourage native plants and creatures of all kinds, both for their own sakes and as objects of study. The author disarmingly describes his own such garden as "an unattractive jungle of plants left to their own devices", but in fact his final sections show that one need not go to quite such extremes if one wants to have a garden that is attractive as well as an encouragement to birds and beasts. In such a way one can aid the conservation of wildlife under increasing pressure in its original habitats.

The interludes and asides about naturalists and natural history in this book provide a refreshingly distinct approach to garden history as Dr Feltwell paints his wide canvas. It is an approach that should remind us that a garden is a microcosm of the natural world, an ecosystem in its own right – knowledge that can enhance our pleasure in our small creation.

Anthony Huxley

*By providing winter food and
spring nesting, you can attract many
different kinds of birds.*

INTRODUCTION

Naturalists have come a long way since Pliny the Naturalist surveyed his respectable gardens from the comfort of his Roman villas. The garden of a present-day naturalist may be indistinguishable from a patch of scrub or woodland.

Throughout the ages the development of gardens has been influenced by men of scientific curiosity. Thanks to their fascination with the natural world, their meticulous observation of the plants and animals that inhabit it and their collection of unique and exotic plants from far-off places, our appreciation of the wonders of life around us has reached a high level of awareness.

A love of flowers and interest in wildlife has found expression in many ways – through poetry and painting as well as in the creation of gardens as sanctuaries of tranquillity and beauty. A naturalist is always alert in the course of his travels to the wonders of the living world, and his garden at home might be a reflection of some of the best habitats he has visited, or an attempt to re-create the perfect environment for the plants of his choice. In the past a dedicated collector such as John Tradescant filled his London garden with exciting New World species. The Mayflower pioneers took their own English seeds with them to start their New World vegetable gardens in the traditional way. Natural history lore was born out of the philosphical debates held in some of the great Italian gardens of the Renaissance, an extension of the wisdom generated by Aristotle and Pliny. Many plants held a religious significance, and medical knowledge was dominated by their medicinal properties. Studying natural history became a gentleman's pastime in which physicians and parsons excelled. Darwin's startling theory of evolution played its part, drawing attention to the vital links between animal and plant life and the survival of man.

But above all the desire to reproduce the natural world in a controlled environment is at the heart of every naturalist's dream: the attempt to turn a piece of wasteland into an oasis for wildlife seems to hold a universal appeal. With our twentieth-century awareness of the need to preserve those habitats that remain and the present-day commitment to nature conservation, there is a strong desire in people to hold on to our beautiful living world, to re-create medieval meadows and re-establish rare plants and wayside weeds and to tempt back into our gardens some of the birds and the butterflies that are in danger of extinction.

To the naturalist, gardens are simply botanical paradises which attract zoological activity. As an antidote to our preoccupation with commercial interests and the indiscriminate use of herbicides, wildlife gardens will help protect life on earth. It is never too late to start.

CHAPTER ONE

GARDENS
OF
ANTIQUITY
(2000 BC – 1485 AD)

Gardens are as old as civilization itself, and the role of naturalists in their creation is of equal antiquity. Our earliest pictures of gardens – the Egyptian tomb paintings – reveal the same fascination with the natural world that we feel today, as do the first written accounts – vivid descriptions by scientists, naturalists and historians that have far outlasted those gardens that first inspired them.

Many of these early observations reveal a surprisingly sophisticated horticultural knowledge. The Greek philosopher, Aristotle, was perhaps the first "naturalist", in that he made detailed observations of wildlife during his two-year study of the wild "gardens" of the island of Lesbos. And his firm belief that the natural world should receive greater scientific attention paved the way for much of what was to follow.

Although information about the gardens of this early period is scarce, evocative descriptions of some of the more ambitious schemes do exist.

A wall painting in Empress Livia's villa at Prima Porta, in ancient Rome.

Four thousand years ago the art of garden making was already well established in Egypt. There were three types of garden: the giant temple gardens, such as the Theban Ammon temple on the banks of the Nile, stretching from Karnac to Luxor and enclosing several square kilometres; the villa gardens of the wealthy, and the smallest of them all, those of the middle classes. We know this from the scroll plans of the earliest Egyptian garden on record, which show a grand villa estate made during the reign of Amenhotep III (ca. 1411-1375 B.C.). It includes vineyards, water lilies, palms and possibly pomegranates. There was no doubt that the Egyptians loved flowers, too, for they spent much of their time growing them for festivals and funerals. They liked bright colours and chose many of the lively coloured species, such as cornflowers and poppies, which are still grown today.

Another of the earliest recorded gardens was that of Queen Hatshepsut's terraced garden at Deir el-Bahri during the second century B.C., which consisted of three terraces containing ornamental ponds and trees with a rock-shrine at the top. Many of her plants were imported and transplanted successfully, suggesting a high standard of horticultural knowledge.

But where were the naturalists at this time? No descriptions of plants and animals have survived. What does exist, however, are pictorial representations of pastoral scenes and wildlife, such as the fresco on the tomb of Thebes, dating from about 1500 B.C., of a cat hunting duck among flowers and butterflies – evidence of the importance the Egyptians attached to the natural world around them. Their love of flowers is well documented, too, in their tomb paintings. In the tomb of Tutankhamun, ruler circa 1333-1323 B.C., are panels depicting garden scenes and varieties of flowers such as lotus and cornflowers, and a small floral wreath was found inside the coffin itself.

Some of the plants the Egyptians grew provided both shade and food, such as the indigenous date and doum palms, and figs. Other large trees such as acacias, tamarisks and shrub mallows provided nectar for honeybees, essential in any large garden for the honey they produced. Other plants had their uses too. One species the Egyptians revered was the so-called lotus flower. This was not the delightful pink lotus from the East, but the yellow and white water lilies (*Nymphaea* spp.) which were picked for ornamental purposes on all occasions. There is a wall painting from a Theban tomb of the fifteenth dynasty showing water lilies being collected. The iris, too, had a prized place in Egyptian gardens.

It was used as a medicinal plant, of sufficient importance for The Pharaoh, Thutmosis I (1540 B.C.), to have it depicted on the walls at Karnac.

The gardens on the banks of the Nile had to be irrigated in this dry and dusty land and the Egyptians were experts at moving water by canal or weighted pole. The Nile at this time was teeming with wildlife and the people were quick to profit from its wealth. Pools were stocked with fish, as fish farms and water fowl were introduced. In the rushes and beds of papyrus – which was used for paper-making – were small crocodiles which would eat the fish, fox-like mammals which disturbed the waterfowl and day-flying moths flitting from one flower to the next.

THE PERSIANS

Admirers of the Egyptian approach to gardening were the Persians, whose own love of plants is embodied in the famous hanging gardens of Babylon, one of the seven wonders of the ancient world. These consisted of a huge seven-storey terraced building festooned with plants. It was said to have looked like a "green mountain" from afar. Reputed to have been built by King Nebuchadnezzar for his wife in about the sixth century B.C., these gardens were described in some detail by Diodorus Siculus, a Greek historian writing at the

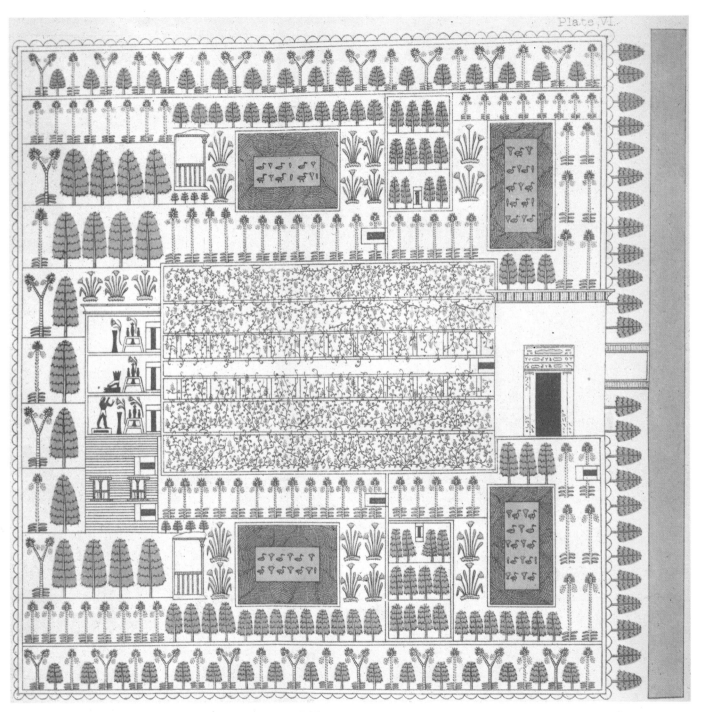

Plate VI.

Left: *Named in Greek after the goddess of springs, these water-lilies (Nymphaea spp.) were the "lotus" plants of ancient Egypt – not the far eastern pink lotus (Nelumbo). The wide variety found today are garden hybrids.*

Above: *A tomb painting of the garden of a high official of Amenhotep III. The central vineyard is flanked by four ponds, stocked with waterfowl and waterlilies. Two of the ponds have adjacent pavilions.*

end of the first century B.C. He, however, attributed their creation to a prince called Cyrus who had built them in the Persian style for his favourite courtesan. Diodorus wrote:

> "This garden was built up in tiers so that it resembled a theatre. Vaults had been constructed under the ascending terraces which carried the entire weight of the planted garden; the uppermost vault, which was 75 ft high, was . . . on the same level as the city walls."

The gardens covered about 1.5 ha (3½ acres) and there were many arches and battlements. Water was stored in a special well and raised to the top in leather buckets. The floor of the highest terrace was waterproofed with layers of papyrus mixed with asphalt, a layer of tiles, bricks and mortar and covered with lead and a layer of topsoil thick enough to allow big trees to thrive. Hanging and trailing plants, such as ivy and vines, provided shade for lower terraces. There may even have been weeping willows; in the 18th century Linnaeus alluded to this source in his Latin name for the species *Salix babylonica*. The local wildlife would have soon adapted to living in these green havens: lizards and geckos would bask on the brickwork, perhaps also the desert monitor, a metre long; small mammals would steal through the undergrowth, water voles frequent the irrigation canals and birds would feed on insects and the fruits of mimosa, birch and aspen. Perhaps, too, kingfishers flew during the day and barn owls at night. Cranes probably nested on some rooftops as they do today.

Water, indispensable in those arid lands, was the chief feature of the Persian garden which traditionally was divided into four parts by water courses fed from a central source. These served to irrigate the plantings of roses and other flowers, shrubs and ornamental trees.

It was during the first millenium B.C. that "parks" were originated, it is believed by the Assyrians. The word comes from the Greek translation of the Persian "pardes". Some of the successful Persian warriors made large parks for their subjects and planted them with enormous numbers of trees, especially the much loved Cedar of Lebanon which they had brought back from campaigns. Trees were so important to the Persians that all young people were encouraged to plant, nurture and respect trees of their own.

NATURALISTS OF GREECE AND ROME

If Egyptian and Persian gardens were a delight to those interested in wild flowers, insects, birds and mammals, the Greeks and Romans excelled in producing some notable naturalists and philosophers who recorded their observations. Aristotle (384-322 B.C.), the Greek philosopher and

Left: An artist's impression of the hanging gardens of Babylon in their heyday. Seen from afar, the soaring and spacious terraces seemed to float in the air.

Below: This Persian carpet clearly illustrates the standard design of the Persian garden. The cartouche in the middle stands for the central pavilion, from which four rivers flow. A broad row of cypresses and fruit trees form the boundary.

tutor to Alexander the Great, was the first to itemize all his observations with meticulous precision. He was an enthusiastic naturalist who spent two years studying the wild "garden" on the island of Lesbos (344-342 B.C.). He also indulged in marine biology, but his natural history masterpiece is his *De Partibus Animalium*, in which he justifies his belief that the natural world should receive greater academic attention. His pupil, Theophrastus, made a close study of plants, and some of his written work on the subject still survives. He listed no less than 450 plants known in Greece at that time.

Ordinary Greek people had their own little gardens, and every year they celebrated the festival of Adonis (in late summer in Athens, in spring elsewhere) by growing seeds of plants such as wheat, barley, lettuce and fennel in tiny baskets, intricately adorned. The plants were grown quickly and allowed to wilt and fade in recognition of the death and resurrection of Adonis who was killed by a wild boar. In spring, the Greek countryside is a spectacle of wild flowers and in late summer everything is dried up, but the Greeks knew how to cultivate the vine, fig and olive in the searing heat.

Gardens and the cultivation of flowers became an important part of Greek life as their knowledge of the achievements of their Egyptian and Persian subjects spread, following the conquests of Alexander the Great in 330 B.C. Towns such as Alexandria in Egypt and Antioch in Syria became renowned for their gardens.

Roman gardens were modelled very much on Greek lines and by the time the Roman Republic became an Empire in 27 B.C. the wealth of its citizens had found expression in

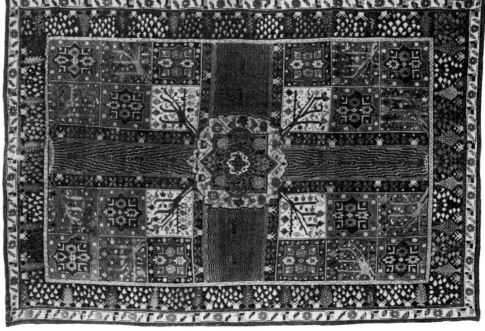

the creation of large estates and hunting parks. Public and private gardens were established in and around their cities with colonnades, statuary, sunken lawns, streams and grottoes, such as that depicted on a fresco at Pompeii, as well as plantations of trees and flowers.

In about 50 A.D. Pedanios Dioscorides, a soldier-physician in Nero's army, wrote a book, *De Materia Medica*, in which he listed almost 600 species of medicinal plants and various animal products which were used medicinally. It could be said that he was the first to establish botany as an applied science, and that the botanical section of his book, which was in five parts, constituted the first herbal. He refers to the early Persians using jasmine oil to perfume the air at their banquets, and he comments disapprovingly about walnuts, suggesting that they caused stomach upsets and headaches and encouraged vomiting, but could be usefully used for fasting. Some people followed his suggestion.

The Emperor Nero (37-68 A.D.) himself was credited with a fine garden. The great fire of Rome in July 64 A.D. has been attributed to Nero, and he certainly used the vast areas of burnt city to set out his magnificent grounds around his Golden House.

Two other great naturalists and gardeners in Roman times were Pliny the Elder (ca 23-79 A.D.), otherwise called Pliny the Naturalist, and his nephew, Pliny the Younger (ca 61-113 A.D.). Pliny the Naturalist was a prodigious writer and his *Historia Naturalis* (probably published in 77 A.D.) runs to 37 volumes. It was dedicated to Jove the chestnut-oak, to Apollo the bay, to Minerva the olive, to Venus the myrtle, and to Hercules the poplar (*UT IOVI AESCULUS, APOLLINI LAURUS, MINERVAE OLEA, VENERI MYRTUS, HERCULI POPULUS*). This give some idea of the tree species being grown at this time.

Pliny's books mention a wide range of plants, such as the typical Mediterranean pine (the stone or umbrella pine,

Cicadas are summer insects typical of the Mediterranean region, where they crowd on to trees and sing when it is very hot, creating an incessant noise. Only the male sings to attract females. Some species live for as long as 17 years underground as nymphs.

Pinus pinea), which was prized in any garden for its elegance in maturity, its prolific shade and its edible nuts; laurel, myrtle and periwinkle, and at least a dozen species of roses. It is interesting that Pliny's tomes refer to some 146 Latin and 327 foreign authors, which indicates the degree of advancement of scientific thought during this period.

Unfortunately, the scientific curiosity of Pliny the Elder led to his death. When Vesuvius erupted in A.D. 79, burying Pompeii, he set off to investigate the source of the volcano and was killed by the fumes.

His nephew continued the tradition of studying wild plants and was a fine gardener, though he did have considerable help – 500 slaves who tended his three gardens, one in Rome, one near the sea at Ostia and the chief one in Tuscany, looking across to the Apennines.

In a letter to Domitius Apollinaris, Pliny has left us with this vivid description of his Tuscany garden:

"My house is on the lower slopes of a hill but commands a good view; it faces mainly south. In front of the colonnade is a terrace laid out with box hedges clipped into figures of animals cut out of box facing each other on either side ... below ... a bed of acanthus so soft one could say it looked like water. All round is a path hedged by bushes which are trained and cut into different shapes – box shrubs clipped into innumerable shapes, some being letters which spell the gardener's name or his master's. The climate in winter is cold and frosty and so quite impossible for myrtles and olives."

The acanthus mentioned here is not the plant we know by that name today, which grows to over 1 m (3 to 4 ft) tall, but a ground-cover plant which may have been some kind of moss or herb. Topiary, the practice of clipping box into various decorative shapes, had become a sophisticated and highly skilled art by Pliny's time. He himself credits Gaius Matius, a friend of the Emperor Augustus, 63 B.C. to A.D. 14, with its invention.

The garden at his villa near Rome, the Laurentum, was relatively simple and verged on the formal, with box topiary figures and rosemary hedges, vine arbours conferring valuable shade, beds of violets (especially white ones) and orchards of figs and mulberries. Cicadas would sing incessantly in the midday heat and crickets chirp in the cool nights. At Pliny's other estate there were more informal groups of sycamore and cypresses with ground cover of acanthus and roses to perfume the shady walks. Lawns were a new invention – areas to think, walk about and do exercises on – but water was always essential in this climate and was featured in artificial streams and fountains.

The wildlife of a Roman garden is portrayed in the wall paintings from the house of Emperor Caesar Augustus's wife Livia. From these it can be seen that the garden was planted

"A doctor holding a 'turtle'", from
Pliny's Historia Naturalis. *Pliny was
one of the earliest writers to draw
attention to the evils of pollution:
"It is not unusual for us to poison
rivers and the very elements of
which the world is made . . ."*

with quince, pomegranate, strawberry tree, oleander and wilder areas with periwinkle and poppies. Song birds nested in the trees and magpies, jays, golden orioles and fly-catchers were frequent visitors. Today the golden oriole is a rare bird in the Mediterranean and hardly ever visits gardens, but spotted fly-catchers still commonly nest in fruit trees up against walls and jays and magpies are very common scavengers in gardens.

ROMAN LEGACIES

The Romans were responsible for the widespread dispersal of many plants and animals throughout Northern Europe, including Britain, in the course of their conquests. Many seeds arrived by accident, carried in clothing and equipment. Even the Roman legionnaire's sandals are thought to have played their part in harbouring alien seeds which fell off on the long marches across country. Lots of common weeds, vegetable crops and orchard trees grown in gardens today owe their presence to the Romans. Coming from the Mediterranean, where much of the natural vegetation of the countryside includes pleasant-smelling herbs like thyme, marjoram and fennel, the Romans naturally brought with them plants such as these, which they were accustomed to use for seasoning in their cooking.

The edible (or grey) dormouse (*Glis glis*), native to a region from southern France to Turkey, was a Roman delicacy and they introduced it to the northern and western areas of their empire. According to Marcus Varro (116-27 B.C.), who wrote in meticulous detail about their husbandry – he kept them at his villa – these dormice were generally housed in earthenware pots and fed on currants and chestnuts. Sometimes they grew too large for their containers and the pots had to be broken to release them. The Romans originally introduced them to England and, in recent years, they were re-introduced by Walter Rothschild (1868-1937) at Tring, north of London in 1902, but they have not colonized much further than that area today.

The edible dormouse still occurs in Mediterranean regions, but the garden dormouse (*Eliomys quercinus*) has a wider distribution (though not in England) and is particularly associated with houses and gardens, climbing well, taking over old birds' nests, and making nests in houses, mines and caves. The common (or hazel) dormouse (*Muscardinus avellanarius*) has a much wider distribution in England than the edible dormouse and frequently hibernates in bird boxes. Also a Roman introduction, the edible snail (*Helix pomatia*), supposedly brought into England as a source of food, still lives today along the North Downs, venturing into gardens to feed on damp leaves.

Another animal associated with the Romans is the fallow deer. These attractive creatures were traded amongst merchants from the Mediterranean, probably before the Romans, by the sea-going Bronze Age and Iron Age Phoenicians. Today feral fallow deer are a nuisance in many areas of Europe and America, stealing into gardens in country districts and especially eating roses.

Left: The restored central tank, garden and peristyle of the House of the Golden Cupids at Pompeii. The garden was decorated with statues and the flower beds were bordered with box.

Left: A delicacy of the Roman table were these Roman snails (Helix pomatia) which still live in southern England, where they were supposedly introduced from Italy.

Above: Hibernating in a curled-up foetal position, the hazel dormouse (Muscardinus avellanarius) sleeps through the winter, living only on its body food reserves.

THE ROSE

The Perfume Makers, *by Rudolph Ernst (1854-1932). The petals of* Rosa centifolia, *the Provence or Cabbage rose, are used for rose perfume.*

One part of a garden which has changed little over the centuries is the rose bed. Roses were grown originally because of their medicinal qualities as a cure-all against a hundred ailments, their religious symbolism and later for their beauty. Apart from harbouring aphids and black spot, the wildlife association of bush roses is small. But there was one feature of the wild rose which was greatly respected by apothecaries and that was the rose pincushion, a feathery red ball of fluff produced by the plant in response to small white grubs of a parasitic wasp embedded in its tissues. These fluffy balls were collected

Above: Robin's pincushion

Left: Dog rose
(*Rosa canina*)

French rose
(*Rosa gallica*)

Provence rose
(*Rose centifolia*)

White rose of York
(*Rosa alba*)

Red rose of Lancaster
(*Rosa gallica officinalis*)

Holy rose
(*Rosa sancta*)

York & Lancaster rose
(*Rosa damascena versicolor*)

in the autumn, ground to a powder and taken in the belief that they would drive away worms. Hung round the neck, they were called 'bedeguars', and were thought to prevent whooping-cough. They were greatly sought after in the wilder parts of gardens.

THE FIRST ROSES

Roses were first cultivated 2,000 years ago by the Chinese. By the time of the Sung Dynasty 900 years ago, 41 species were grown in China. The only roses available to the Europeans were the native rose bushes gathered from the countryside – the *Rosa canina* or dog (that is, common) rose. Charlemagne (742-814 A.D.), the Roman Emperor and King of the Franks, was reputed to be an enthusiastic gardener and must have had a keen eye for natural history, since at least 60 species of plant were listed in his gardens, one of which was *Rosa gallica*. This is the "French Rose"; the variety *R.g. officinalis* with semi-double light crimson flowers is the Apothecaries' Rose or Red Rose of Lancaster. *Rosa gallica* was also the main parent of the numerous shrub roses which were developed later.

People of Mediterranean countries always delight in colourful roses and find them a challenge to grow in the intense heat. The Egyptians, with their water-carrying slaves, are known to have valued *Rosa sancta*, and in the Grecian Midas gardens of the fifth century B.C. *Rosa centifolia*, the Provence or Cabbage Rose, so named because of its globular shape, was grown. In the Roman gardens of Pliny the Younger and Livia, for instance, and in the Spanish Moorish gardens such as the Alhambra, roses were grown especially for their fragrant perfume. Pliny is said to have cultivated 12 species of rose. The Persians held the rose in even higher esteem. It is used as a symbol in much Persian literature, particularly in the Omar Khayyam, and Persian mosques were tiled with flowery scenes.

In England, too, the rose was a symbol which meant life or death to many who fought in the War of the Roses between the House of York and the House of Lancaster. Henry VII (1457-1509) joined his own red Lancastrian rose, *Rosa gallica*, with the White Rose of York, *Rosa alba*, when he married Elizabeth of York in 1486, and it was a combination of these two roses which gave rise to the Union or Tudor rose, emblem of the House of Tudor. Even today the regimental colours of the Royal Hampshire Regiment use the rose as an emblem.

High on the list of the legionnaire's important plants were medicinal ones, renowned for their "virtues", or powers to treat diseases. Fennel, rosemary and thyme, familiar wild plants growing on the limestones of the Mediterranean, were harnessed for cultivation in the garden and remain favourites today. Parsley was also used by the Romans to flavour foods. They were not the first to have herb gardens, however. The Greeks before them knew the virtues of all their plants, as Dioscorides demonstrated.

Weeds such as scarlet pimpernel, swine-cress, small buttercups and sow-thistles have always made a nuisance of themselves in gardens and others such as ground elder (*Aegopodium podagraria*), now a pernicious garden weed, was brought in as an important medicinal plant against gout and used as a vegetable, for the leaves can be boiled down like spinach. Gardens sported species such as field woundwort (*Stachys arvensis*), field spurrey, hemlock (*Conium maculatum*), and corn marigold, some of which had escaped from corn fields. It is interesting that species like Scotch thistle and corncockle (*Agrostemma githago*), which were present in Roman times as wild flowers, are now grown as ornamental garden plants, and their seeds are sold in shops. Corncockle was later destined to create a nuisance in the flour mills, as its crushed seeds gave a bad taste to bread and caused gastro-enteritis.

The orchards of which Pliny the Younger wrote were a useful and productive part of a typical villa estate, though few people had an orchard or even an apple tree in their gardens. The art of grafting and growing trees as espaliers had been pioneered by the Egyptians long before the Romans used it. Figs, pears, apples and damsons were grown around the cabbages, leeks, onions, garlic and lettuce in the earliest kitchen gardens belonging to the wealthy. Peaches had come originally from China but the precise date for their introduction to the West is not known, though it seems likely that the Romans imported peaches directly from Asia.

One of the main fruits introduced widely into northern Europe and attributed to the Romans is the apple, a fruit with a varied and interesting history. It is thought to have originated from as many as 25 wild species found in the region where Russia, Turkey and Iran meet. Here two species, *Malus pumila* (whose fruit has a sweet taste) and *M. sylvestris*, the crab apple with a sour taste, may have been the nearest ancestors from which thousands of varieties have been cultivated ever since, many by grafting. Seventeen centuries later the European colonists to America took with them only apple seeds, rather than grafted plants. This gave their apples a greater genetic variety and has resulted in the differences between present-day European and American apples.

MOORISH AND MEDITERRANEAN GARDENS

The Persian style of garden, with its emphasis on water and love of flowers and trees, was assimilated by the Arabs whose power spread widely in the wake of Rome's decline.

*One of several colourful cornfield weeds, the corncockle (*Agrostemma githago*) joined pink scabious, red corn poppies, yellow corn marigolds and blue cornflowers in playing havoc with our crops. Now removed by seed-cleaning techniques and herbicides, these are species which naturalists are trying to re-establish.*

Their influence was carried as far west as North Africa, Sicily and Spain.

The Moors arrived in southern Spain from North Africa in the early part of the eighth century and their influence lasted until 1492. They cultivated many species of plant, including citrus trees, jasmine, palms, oleanders, irises, narcissi and spiraeas. Only plenty of water was necessary to sustain a garden under the glorious Spanish sunshine. Constant animal visitors would have been cicadas, geckos, butterflies and black redstarts, just as they are today.

In Cordoba, southern Spain, is the oldest garden in Europe, the Patio de los Naranjos, which was created in 976 A.D. by Al-Mansur. The Moorish influence is most strongly reflected, however, in the perfectly balanced blend of architecture and garden design in the Alhambra of Granada. Built by Christian slaves between 1238 and 1354 for Mohammed ben Alhamar, it covered a 14 ha (34½ acres) site on a plateau overlooking Granada, the capital of the Province of Granada in southern Spain. It is laid out on a grand scale and some of the names of its parts reflect the interest in wildlife: the courtyard of the myrtles; the pomegranate gate; the court of the lions – all fairly local species at that period. The Moorish park, complete with roses, orange groves and myrtles, was laid out on the plain below. Some 400 years later it was planted with English elms by the Duke of Wellington (1769-1852).

It is not only the park which indicates a Persian influence, but the little arches of vines and cypresses over the paths, and the courtyard for the harem with its tall cypresses and orange trees also reveal its origins. Historically, these are some of the earliest walled gardens to survive and they owe their existence to the water which was specially diverted to sustain them. As the Greek historian and traveller Herodotus (484-425 B.C.) remarked, "Egypt was a gift of the Nile", so the Alhambra is dependent upon the waters of the Darro river.

Left: *The Alhambra in Granada still retains many of its early, Moorish features.*

Above: *Citrus trees (Citrus spp.) originated in China and were brought to Spain by Arab traders. They soon became a necessary part of Mediterranean gardens. Fruiting well in this warm climate the flowers and fruits grow side by side on the same tree, the fruits taking a year to develop after petal drop.*

The Muslims liked to have different courtyards to retreat to, and above the Alhambra are the gardens of the Generalife, consisting of a series of courts, which still survive. Because of their lovely situation on the side of a hill, these gardens are considered to be the most beautiful of those in the Moorish style. According to Hernando de Baeza, the odd military-sounding name is thought to mean, "the greatest and grandest of all orchards". A Spanish folk song refers to it as "an orchard which had no equal".

Water features prominently in the overall design, as can be seen from a description written in 1526 by a visiting Venetian nobleman: "It has many courts, all abundantly supplied with water, but one in particular with a canal running through the middle and full of fine orange trees and myrtles . . ."

To the devout, the gardens at Alhambra were symbolic of what the Koran speaks of as an Islamic paradise garden, "a luxuriant garden covered in shadowy-green, cooled by water streams, and with fruit, pomegranate and palm trees, where the blessed, on green brocade rugs and cushions, rest leisurely inside pavilions surrounded by heavenly houris (sic) and youths". Indeed the gardens were a delicious oasis in the burning soils of southern Spain. The many verdant courtyards suggested to Fernando de Pulgar in 1238 that "it should be regarded rather more like a town than a fortress and royal palace".

THE MONASTIC INFLUENCE

The Moorish gardens were the most sophisticated in Europe at this time and up to the end of the fifteenth century. For the rest of Europe this was a period with precious little information on gardening or about any naturalists, although there must have been individual enthusiasts.

In the Dark Ages following the collapse of the Roman Empire it was the monks who kept the knowledge of medicinal plants alive, and they had to be self-supporting in growing their own fruit, vegetables and herbs. The open-sided cloisters surrounding an enclosed courtyard were, perhaps, a legacy of the Roman style of architecture but here in this area of peace and shelter the monks would cultivate their vegetables and grow their herbs and flowers. There were monastic gardens in England both at Ely, Norfolk, and Canterbury, Kent, in the twelfth century and there the secrets of medicinal plants were certainly known.

The English monks introduced two plants which were to become the ancestors of garden pinks and carnations, the clove pink, *Dianthus caryophyllus*, and the common pink, *D. plumarius*, both from south-west France. Flowers were grown for their symbolic meanings, especially roses and lilies: white ones symbolized the purity of the Virgin Mary, while red ones represented Christ's blood, the sign of martyrdom. These were grown in monastic gardens for decoration in

Left: Meadow clary (Salvia pratensis) *grows in damp meadows. The seeds were traditionally uised for removing pieces of dirt from the eye – thus "clary", from "clear eye". Today it is restricted in its range and protected in some reserves. The flowers of clary are so evolved that they attract insects for pollination.*

Right: *The physic garden and vegetable plot (below) and the cemetery (above) from the St Gall plan, Switzerland, for a projected ideal monastery (c. 816-20).*

places of worship.

As the wealth of the monasteries increased and their estates expanded, large areas were set apart outside the walls for the growth of vineyards and fruit. There is, unfortunately, very little alternative evidence of the nature of the medieval garden in Britain. No pictures exist of British gardens of this period, and recorded information is extremely scarce. John Harvey's recent researches into medieval manuscripts, however, show that at least 250 plant species were grown between 800 and 1540. Most of the records refer to gardens on the Continent, yet Friar Henry Daniel grew about that number in his garden at Stepney, London, and Alexander Neckham listed about 140 species in *De Naturis Rerum* and *De Laudibus Divinae Sapientiae*, before 1200.

It was not until the middle of the fifteenth century when gardening for pleasure was still in its infancy that Britain's first gardening book was published. Mayster Jon Gardener's *Feate of Gardening*, published in 1440, listed 97 plants, many of which are familiar in gardens today: cowslips and primroses, daffodils, hollyhocks, honeysuckle and lavender. It is written as a definitive text by an expert and is full of practical advice about planting and grafting trees, when to sow seeds (St Valentine's Day, February 14), the kinds of "worts" – medicinal plants – and sorts of parsley to grow. Other plants which are more at home in wilder gardens today and were present then were foxglove, periwinkle and scabious. Apart from the Roman vegetables already established, there were turnips, radishes and spinach and the herbs grown were borage, clary (the seeds were a specific for clear eyes), camomile, comfrey, mint, rue, sage and southernwood.

There have been several attempts to recreate medieval gardens relying on monastic records. The famous gardens of Château Villandry in the Loire Valley of France combine typical monastic medieval elements, such as the crosses used in their layout, with grander Renaissance elements.

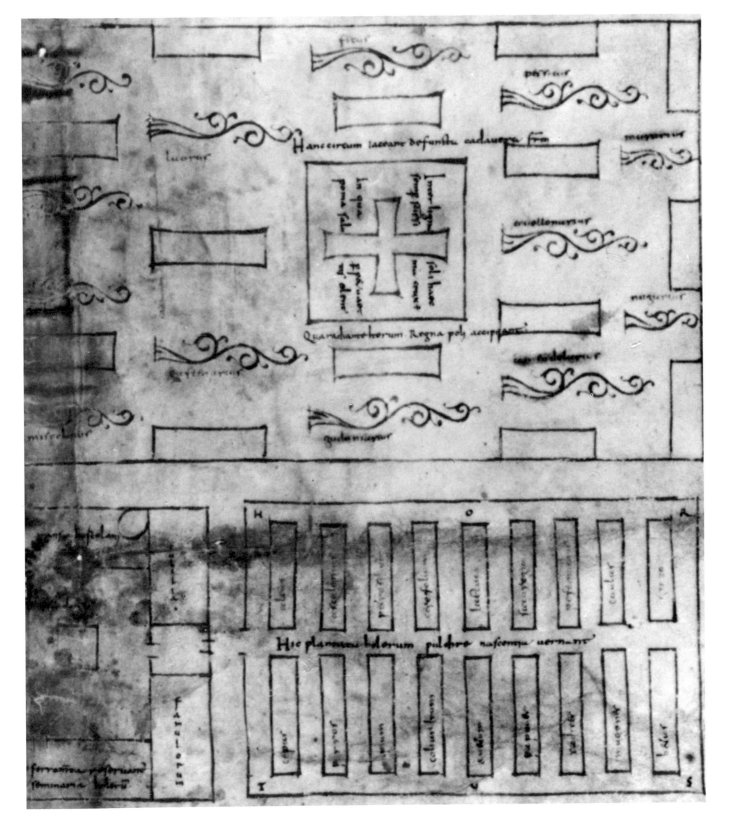

The gardens were already well established in 1570 when the Cardinal of Aragon wrote to the Pope saying that the salad crops produced were better than those grown in Rome. Medieval manuscripts of vegetable gardens prepared by monks in the abbey of Solesmes, near Le Mans, France, were followed closely in the present-day reconstruction at Villandry, and the effect is staggering.

The monks were great naturalists, blending wild flowers with their cultivated crops. Decorative, scented and medicinal plants were grown, too. Some of their vegetables and culinary herbs were indeed wild flowers, such as celery, rosemary, marjoram and borage, and the industrious monks were keen to try new species. At Villandry they planted standards of red and pink roses (again, symbolic colours) between the trim beds of vegetables. The rose bowers and vine arbours made a pleasant distraction from all the hard work which had to be done in a kitchen garden and would have made a fine backdrop to an old château.

Inevitably, the secrets of monastic and château gardening spread to ordinary manor houses and cottage gardens.

A typical Norman farmhouse and courtyard in France or England would have been a naturalist's dream: mosses, ferns, lichens and flowering plants, such as greater celandine (wartwort) growing on and around the stone walls. Song birds, pigeons and sparrows would clean the yard of spilt grain and butterflies flew around the kitchen garden. In the wet meadows snipe and swans sought sanctuary, while among the colourful meadow flowers of summer there would have been a chorus of crickets and grasshoppers. Dippers and kingfishers would have flown along the brook and the farm or village pond would be regularly visited by heron, mallard and teal. In the summer the swallows and house martins would swoop low into the barns and even nest in the house. The odd corner may have supported the poisonous henbane (*Hyoscyamus niger*). The wild woods of England would have sounded to the movement of wild boars just as they do in much of France today. The Normans taught the English a lot about hunting and about keeping deer in parks, but of course the wild boar has long been extinct in Britain. The British also learned from the

Normans how to look after rabbits, especially in warrens, and it was several centuries before rabbits became firmly established in the countryside.

EUROPEAN DEVELOPMENTS

We have a good idea from oil paintings what the gardens of fortified manors in France were like in the twelfth to fifteenth centuries. Many colourful wild plants were carefully dug up from the woods and meadows and put in gardens. Not until the Victorian era would plants be wantonly uprooted from the wild with such fervour. The chalk-loving columbine, or aquilegia, made this journey to the garden, where it has subsequently become more abundant than in its wild state. A sixteenth-century painting of a French castle shows blue and albino forms of columbine growing outside the castle walls amongst the red firebug insects – a true bug which sucks the juice from tree fruits such as lime and is common even today in gardens in the south of France.

The wild tricolor violet, primroses, snowdrops and purple crocuses of the spring meadows were dug up as well as campanulas and lilies of the valley from the woods. The impressive Cedar of Lebanon (*Cedrus libani*) was brought back to Europe for the first time by the Crusaders and

was to become the centrepiece of many fine gardens throughout Europe. Hollyhocks, too, were brought in from eastern Turkey and Persia.

Some of the larger palatial gardens of Italy in the middle of the fourteenth century had both large and small mammals and domestic animals roaming semi-wild. A villa in the hills near Florence was described as supporting rabbits, hares, grazing fawns and kids. These gardens were for the indulgence of the rich only; down in the valley the average Florentine was having to contend with the ravages of plague. Peacocks, partridges and pheasants were also bred for the table and ran wild in enclosed gardens; the song of blackbirds, goldfinches, linnets and nightingales was a naturalist's delight and of great inspiration to the illustrators of illuminated manuscripts.

In the dawn of the Renaissance the art of garden making had reached a high degree of sophistication in Italy, with intricate parterre designs and complex topiary. An illuminating description of the plants then grown is given in an allegorical romance by a Dominican monk named Francesco Colonna, published in 1467, called the *Hypnorotomachia*. The book describes a series of gardens, woods and meadows of "a thousand different flowers" and is illustrated with woodcuts, from which it is clear that a wide range of native plants were in use at that time.

Left: Following ancient plans, the delightful gardens of Villandry re-create the functional monastic gardens full of useful herbs, vegetables and fruit interplanted with highly symbolic blood-red roses – all within sight of the castle so that progress could always be assessed. A different crop is grown in each small bed, edged with box (Buxus *spp.*).

Right: The Garden of Paradise *(c. 1415), by a master from the Upper Rhine. This delightfully detailed painting provides a fascinating glimpse into a medieval garden.*

MEDICINAL
AND
POISONOUS PLANTS

From the period of the Roman Empire through medieval times to the end of the sixteenth century the principal plants grown in gardens were those suitable for eating or for use as medicine. Some of the medicinal plants were, in fact, highly poisonous; their active ingredients which were effective in minute proportions would kill in larger doses. The gardeners who looked after the great gardens belonging to the castles, abbeys and manors knew how to use these plants wisely. There were occasions when their knowledge of botany – we would call it chemotaxonomy today – would be put to good use.

The contents of a typical medieval garden reflected the needs of the day – garlic to flavour rotten meat; dye plants for colouring illuminated manuscripts and cloth (black mulberries); plants to kill off your enemies (monkshood – it looks innocuous in the border); plants for potions to aid conception and ease childbirth (birthwort); to comfort children, dull toothache or earache and eliminate piles (pilewort or lesser celandine); as a remedy for coughs (coltsfoot) and to combat fleas and bed-bugs (fleawort) and lice (lousewort). Plants played a highly important part in the life of people, for food, to combat disease or to support their religious beliefs.

Only women of rich families would have had time to appreciate nature for its own sake. They spent much of their day in the garden, leaving their servants to attend to the daily chores. Their appreciation and observation of living things would be expressed in embroidery in formalized design. Ever since Roman times, men had used the grounds of their castles as somewhere to rest and plan in between campaigns, showing little interest in the study of plants and animals.

Wild plants were given local names and were well known for their medicinal "virtues". Villagers were much better botanists than we are today, since their knowledge had been handed down through generations. They knew all about their local plants – which ones were useful and which were poisonous. Much of this botanical history has been lost since it was not written down and the early herbals, such as John Gerard's

A lady weaving a floral tapestry, from a fifteenth-century Dutch illuminated manuscript. Ornamental horticulture was a popular medieval tapestry theme.

Herball, published in 1597, were none too reliable. It was not until the eighteenth century that a proper system of classified Latin names was given to plants and animals, but we can gather some information in hindsight from the use of the word *"officinalis"* in the Latin names of plants, since this means one of medicinal importance.

MEDICINAL PLANTS

People relied heavily upon local and traded plants for keeping healthy in medieval times – there was no alternative. The most coveted medicinal plants were cosseted in gardens, while others were picked in the wild. By a process of trial and error through the centuries many ordinary plants of the wayside and woodland were found to be of value: borage, as a tonic; bugloss, to ease lumbago; comfrey, as a leaf crop, and eyebright, for which Gerard claimed: "It preserveth the sight, increases it, and being feeble and lost it restorith the same." Lungwort was believed to relieve lung conditions, valerian was used as a tonic, especially in Germany, and in southern Europe marigolds were recommended for skin complaints. Melilot was used as a dye and both Pliny and Dioscorides recommended balm to alleviate melancholy.

Saffron crocuses were grown so extensively for their yellow stamens that places were named after them – Saffron Walden in England, Safranbolu in Turkey and Krokos in Greece. The Egyptians, Romans and the English monks traded in saffron which was sometimes worth its own weight in gold. Fifteenth-century traders in Nuremburg were even burned alive for adulterating saffron. It was not only a natural food colourer and flavourer but was believed to be important for good health. In the present century it has been found to be the richest natural source of vitamin B2.

Comfrey and the propolis collected by honeybees – a sticky resin found in the buds of trees – were becoming established as cure-alls, or to ward off evil spirits. How much "eye of a newt, claw of a lizard" medicine was concocted by European witch doctors we shall never know.

POISONOUS PLANTS

There was plague to contend with, and medieval villages throughout Europe were beset with "Holy Fire", a horrible disease where limbs, fingers and toes turned blue and fell off. One epidemic killed 11,000 people in Russia in medieval times. We now know that the people were dying from ergotamine poisoning because their bread was contaminated. The ergot fungus still grows today on our barley, oats, rye and wheat, as well as on wild grasses, but we operate stringent controls to eliminate it. When milled with the flour the fungus released its deadly poisons.

Many villagers spent a lot of time with their grazing animals, sheep, goats and swine, so they knew very well all the poisonous wild plants such as henbane, ragwort and deadly nightshade. Some of these were put to good use and perhaps were even grown in court-yard gardens, away from children's prying eyes, for the sake of their beautiful colours. In any case, extracts of some of these poisonous plants were found to have a healing effect when used in very small amounts, a characteristic still utilized today and the basis of homeopathic treatment. The poisonous plants were also occasionally used as a surreptitious means of eliminating enemies. An apocryphal story is told of monks bringing back the deadly monkshood (*Aconitum napellus*) from Europe especially for this purpose.

Saffron crocus
(*Crocus sativus*)

Betony
(*Stachys officinalis*)

Common mallow
(*Malva sylvestris*)

Sweet violet
(*Viola odorata*)

Henbane
(*Hyoscyamus niger*)

Ergot fungus
(*Claviceps purpurea*)

Deadly nightshade
(*Atropa belladonna*)

Monkshood
(*Aconitum napellus*)

CHAPTER TWO

MOATS
AND
MOUNTS
(1485 – 1550)

Τhis was an exciting period of exploration and discovery. European travellers were venturing further afield, returning home with many new species of plants to enrich their villa estates or manor gardens. As interest in horticulture grew, specialist botanic gardens were created, where plants could be studied in greater detail.

Garden design became far more sophisticated. The grand Renaissance style was adopted by many of the great houses of Europe. In England, the end of the Wars of the Roses ushered in a period of peace and prosperity in which the manor garden blossomed. The small, functional castle "plot" gave way to more ambitious planting schemes and the creation of many special effects, such as colourful knot gardens, elaborate mazes and artificial "mounts". The fashion for "mounts" was restricted to royalty and the wealthiest landowners. From the tops of these man-made mountains, proud owners could admire the captive "living worlds" they had created below.

Lovers in a formal garden, from a late fifteenth-century French manuscript.

Fundamental changes in gardening which were to have radical effects elsewhere were taking place in Italy in the fifteenth century. The small gardens with the rectangular shape of the monastic cloister characteristic of medieval Europe were giving way to the gardens of the great estates, planned by architects and designers. These were gardens in which to appreciate the living world, to walk along cool, shaded terraces with fountains playing and wild birds singing. Gone were most of the small, purely functional gardens supplying food and herbs, though many persisted as medicinal gardens attached to the universities. Some, such as those at Leyden and Montpellier, remain in existence today.

GARDENS OF THE RENAISSANCE

We catch a glimpse of early Renaissance gardens through the writings of Leone Battista Alberti (1404-72). The influence of Pliny is clearly seen in his recommendation that the house should be built on a slope with "all the Pleasures and Conveniences of Air, Sun and fine Prospects". He writes of the enclosed garden within a roomy courtyard with portico, decorated walls and paving, and favoured the use of topiary and trees which "ought to be planted in Rows exactly even, and answering to one another exactly upon straight Lines." Grottoes, too, were inevitably part of the design with cool, plashing fountains and statuary of nymphs and figures from classical mythology. "The Ancients used to dress the Walls of their Grottoes and Caverns with all manner of rough Work." It is difficult to believe there can have been any place for wildlife in this well-ordered scene – a mole, pigeon or squirrel in the wrong place would hardly have been tolerated.

This emphasis on the desirability of building on a slope to gain a "fine prospect" is a central theme to many of the great gardens of the Renaissance, but it is not until later in the period that garden statuary came to play such a vital part and a true appreciation of garden architecture was developed, and the natural resources of the landscape were fully exploited. An early example of this principle is illustrated well in the gardens of the Villa Medici in Rome, where a staircase screened by greenery climbs to the top of a mount and suddenly there is revealed a breathtaking view of the city below, all the more effective because it is unexpected.

With the development of trade and the increase in travel and urbanization came greater wealth for certain sections of the population, and it was from the accumulated riches of these families that many of the noble gardens came into being. Such was the background of the powerful Medici family, and one of the most famous of the grand gardens of the period was the Villa Careggi outside Florence. It was created in 1457 by Michelozzo Michelozzi for Cosimo de' Medici who used it for meetings of the Platonic Academy and it became an intellectual centre in Europe. This rich, regulated green environment provided a setting conducive to much philosophical debate. The walled garden was classical in design with fountains incorporating sculptures, lemon houses from which the citrus trees would be carried out in pots for the summer, espalier fruit trees, pergolas with jasmine – a recent arrival from the East Indies – and a secret garden which would include beds of herbs. Holm oaks, myrtles and bay trees provided shade. Still in the medieval tradition, the garden was rectangular in shape and there were pools, with ornamental fountains and lawns on which games could be played.

Cosimo also had a medieval garden containing small beds of flowers and vegetables at his villa estate Cafaggiolo in the cooler hills overlooking Florence. The philosophers were keen gardeners and liked to grow new trees and shrubs from abroad. Lorenzo de' Medici (Lorenzo the Magnificent, 1449-92), Cosimo's grandson, took a particular interest in the new plants grown at Careggi and brought the two subjects of art and natural history together, sponsoring a painting academy at the San Marco gardens.

From philosophy, with its roots going back to Aristotle and Pliny, a study of natural history gradually evolved. These large and formal gardens were big enough to allow the animal life of the countryside to steal in – birds, lizards, small mammals and insects – and in fact they were deliberately encouraged. The gentlemen dabbled in falconry, fishing and feasting within their large estates and gardens. There were large plantations of white mulberry trees to satisfy the hungry silkworms, for Italy had known the secret of producing silk since the tenth century when Roger, King of Sicily, had kidnapped a group of Greek silk weavers when he sacked Corinth in AD 947. Mulberry trees were grown as orchards and their leaves laboriously collected for the caterpillars, which have insatiable appetites. As in the large Medici Villa Poggio a Caiano near Florence, there were walled gardens, lemon houses and beds of medicinal herbs.

Left: *The stairway to the mount at the Villa Medici in Rome. The mount was circular and enclosed with cypresses, cut into the shape of a fortress with a pavilion.*

Above: *Growing in damp and shady woods, especially in limestone areas, the hart's tongue fern (Phyllitis scolopendrium) has attractive unbranched fronds which unfurl upwards like a bishop's crozier. It is an attractive wild plant, frequently growing on garden walls and banks. During summer months spores are produced from the undersides of the fronds.*

Another impressive garden was Villa Castello, decribed by Vasari as "the most rich, magnificent and ornamental garden in Europe". It was noted for its recently introduced trees and flowering plants, such as jasmine from the East Indies.

The full splendour of the spirit of the Renaissance age was realized in the Villa Belvedere, designed for Pope Julius II by Bramante, who died in 1514 before the work was completed. Bramante achieved a magical blend of architecture and landscape in perfect proportion by using the art of perspective in a way that had never been seen before, creating terraces, ramps and staircases and deploying statuary in a manner still used in garden design today. Visiting the garden in 1523, the Venetian ambassador wrote:

"One enters a very beautiful garden of which half is filled with growing grass and bays, mulberries and cypresses, while the other half is paved with squares of bricks laid upright, and in every square a beautiful orange tree grows out of the pavement, of which there are a great many arranged in perfect order. In the centre of the garden are two enormous men of marble, one is the Tiber, the other the Nile, very ancient figures, and two fountains issue from them . . . As high off the ground as an altar, opposite a most perfect well, is the Laocoon . . . Not far from this, mounted in a similar fashion, is the Venus . . . On one side of the garden is a most beautiful loggia, at one end of which is a lovely fountain that irrigates the orange trees and the rest of the garden by a little canal in the centre of the loggia."

Frost-sensitive olive trees (Olea europaea) become gnarled and twisted with holes in their trunks as they age. Their silvery-grey leaves are evergreen and their fruits have supported the economy of several nations.

BESIDE THE MEDITERRANEAN

Oranges and other citrus plants had a profound impact on the style of gardening in Southern Europe. Oranges and lemons were certainly present in Moorish Spain when the Courtyard of the Orange Trees was laid out in the mosque at Cordoba in AD 974 – probably the oldest enclosed garden in Europe. Other citrus seeds were carried from China to southern Italy before 1500 along the silk route through India. In south-east Asia there are still wild citrus plants such as the pummelo (*Citrus maxima* or *grandis*), ancestor of the grapefruit, which are used as genetic resources for new crops.

The advantage of a Mediterranean climate is that many more frost-susceptible plants such as citrus and olive trees can be grown. If water sources can be controlled, Mediterranean gardens will flourish. Sweet chestnuts and oleander (in its white, pink and red forms) would have been grown in the fifteenth and sixteenth centuries beside the Mediterranean.

The grand gardens of southern Europe had plenty of room for shady arbours, walks and fruit trees. Naturalists living around the Mediterranean never had to encourage wildlife in their gardens: it was always there, colourful and noisy, from golden orioles, casual visitors to gardens, to cicadas, incessant in their noise (it is only the male which sings), they crowd on to tree trunks in July, sometimes twenty per tree. The olive groves and citrus avenues would have been flowery paradises extending into the hills around the towns and villages. Snakes, lizards and colourful bee-eaters which nest in sandy cliffs would have been constant visitors. The peasant could enjoy the flowers of the countryside that he tilled – orchids, scabiouses, campanulas, campions and a wide range of scented herbs. Many of these, such as thyme, rosemary, fennel and lavender, were brought into the garden for culinary purposes.

Olive trees have always been an essential part of any garden and village in the Mediterranean since they are native to virtually the entire coast except that of northern Egypt. A useful tree, the olive provides shade and produces edible fruits which can be crushed to make oil, the most widely used basis for cooking throughout the Mediterranean countries. Individual trees will live for several centuries. The silvery evergreen leaves rustle in the wind and hide the tiny serin in its quest for insects; scorpions may be found resting in the gnarled bark.

Left: *Bramante designed the Villa Medici garden in Fiesole, built as a series of interlocking terraces.*

Above: *The delicate mauve flowers of the wild-growing teasel (Dipsacus spp.) attract the commonest swallowtail of the Mediterranean (Iphiclides podalirius). Old spiky teasel heads were once used to fluff out wool.*

For Greece, the olive has been the cash crop and salvation of its economy for thousands of years. The village of Knossos, in Crete, must have been surrounded by tens of thousands of hectares of olive groves, since its massed pots, an archaeological relic, indicate that it had the capacity for storing over 350,000 litres (77 gal.) of olive oil. And the wildlife potential of olive groves is immense. Cornfield weeds grow freely here and between the rows of olives in the sixteenth century there would have been a colourful scene of red corn poppy and pheasant's eye (*Adonis* spp.), pink corn cockle (*Agrostemma githago*), yellow corn marigold (*Chrysanthemum segetum*), blue in various shades with cornflower, chicory and Venus's looking glass (*Specularia*). There would have been colourful displays of the scarce swallowtail butterflies – those are the ones which appear to fly backwards since their long "tails" look like antennae – and a multitude of skipper butterflies.

Orange and lemon trees grow quite well outside but are susceptible to frost and will only fruit in the very warmest areas of the Riviera. Further north the trees were kept in pots and brought inside for the winter.

Like oranges and lemons the pomegranate bears both flowers and fruits on the plant at the same time, this year's flowers with last year's fruits. The large, bell-shaped orangey-red flowers of the pomegranate are far more striking than the small cream citrus flowers and it was not surprising that it was such a favourite in gardens; perhaps the ruddy colour of the petals was considered symbolic of its healing powers over wounds.

Today it is a naturalized plant in many gardens in southern Europe, though it is a native of South and West Asia. It is as vigorous and prickly to have in the garden as a bramble; when cut down it grows up to two metres (six feet) in a year. Also known as the Libyan or Carthaginian apple, it has a long ancestry in the garden, from Egyptian and Roman times, when it was endowed with numerous medicinal virtues, especially for treating tapeworms. In North Africa its bark and fruit rind were used for dyeing leather. When John Tradescant (1603-62) brought it back to England it was quite a novelty and lovingly cared for in gardens.

DEVELOPMENT OF TUDOR GARDENING

As with other cultural achievements of the Renaissance age, the grand Italian style of gardening spread through Europe and soon reached England. Unfortunately many fine medieval gardens were destroyed at the time of Henry VIII's dissolution of the monasteries, denying us the knowledge of their secrets. The Italian idea of having various forms of birds and mammals sculptured in stone and displayed at different parts of the garden, as in a *trompe l'oeil*, was adopted in other grand gardens in Europe, and can still be seen in many of the magnificent gardens of French châteaux and English stately homes today. It was fashionable to display around the garden one's favourite wild animals petrified in stone, in celebration of the real thing – "the chase" was a male indulgence. The flower gardens were for the ladies.

In 1533 Henry VIII extended his gardens at Hampton

*Two typical Mediterranean plants, the Venus's looking glass (*Specularia, spp., left*) and pomegranate (*Punica granatum, right*) both flower in the spring. The bright colours of Venus's looking glass stand out in the poor soils used for cultivation. The blood-red seeds of pomegranate were used by the Greeks for removing tapeworms, but with their bright colour were considered to be highly symbolic, too. Like citrus, pomegranate produces its fruits and flowers together.*

GARDEN PLANTS
INTRODUCED TO ENGLAND BEFORE 1550

Alexanders (*Smyrnium olusatrum*)
Alkanet (*Anchusa* spp.)
Almond *Prunus dulcis*)
Apple mint (*Mentha rotundifolia*)
Angelica (*Angelica archangelica*)
Asarabacca (*Asarum europaeum*)

Balm (*Melissa officinalis*)
Birthwort (*Aristolochia clematitis*)
Blue-eyed Mary
  (*Omphalodes verna*)
Borage (*Borago officinalis*)

Feverfew.

Caper spurge (*Euphorbia lathyrus*)
Caraway (*Carum carvi*)
Catmint (*Nepeta catari*)
Chinese lantern (*Physalis alkekengi*)
Creeping bellflower
  (*Campanula rapunculoides*)
Cypress spurge
  (*Euphorbia cyparissias*)

Dame's violet (*Hesperis matronalis*)
Dusky cranesbill
  (*Geranium phaeum*)

Elecampane (*Inula helenium*)

Feverfew
  (*Chrysanthemum parthenium*)

Greater leopard's bane
  (*Doronicum pardalianches*)

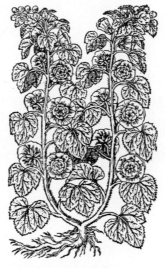

Hieraceum aurantiacum
Hollyhock (*Althaea rosea*)
Hyssop (*Hyssopus officinalis*)

Laburnum (*Laburnum anagyroides*)
Lungwort (*Pulmonaria* spp.)
Leopard's bane
  (*Doronicum plantagineum*)

Mint (*Mentha* spp.)
Moth mullein (*Verbascum blattaria*)

Norway maple (*Acer platanoides*)

Opium poppy
  (*Papaver somniferum*)

Opium poppy.

Peach-leaved bell-flower
  (*Campanula persicifolia*)
Pennyroyal (*Mentha pulegium*)
Periwinkle (*Vinca minor*)
Pink spiraea (*Spiraea salicifolia*)
Purple corydalis (*Corydalis solida*)

Soapwort

Red orache (*Atriplex hortensis rubra*)
Rue (*Ruta graveolens*)

Saffron crocus (*Crocus sativus*)
Sage (*Salvia officinalis*)
Savory (*Satureia hortensis*)
Scarlet-berried elder
  (*Sambucus racemosa*)
Scots pine, long-leaved variety
  (*Pinus sylvestris*)
Sedum reflexum
Snapdragon (*Antirrhinum majus*)
Soapwort (*Saponaria officinalis*)
Sweet alyssum (*Lobularia maritima*)

Variegated deadnettle
  (*Lamium maculatum aureum*)

White butterbur (*Petasites albus*)
White poplar (*Populus alba*)
White woodrush (*Luzula luzuloides*)
Woad (*Isatis tinctoria*)

Yellow anemone
  (*Anemone ranunculoides*)

were fixed on poles throughout his garden. This royal practice is not entirely forgotten since the Queen's beasts, carefully trimmed in yew, were planted on the occasion of Queen Elizabeth I's coronation at Hall Place in Bexley, Kent.

Henry also built a palace and gardens at Nonsuch in what is now south-west London (nothing of the palace survives today) and modelled it upon Italian designs used at the recently built Fontainbleau near Paris. The gardens also contained wild woods, clearings, a maze, hedges and flower beds – a new departure from the small medieval gardens of old.

But not all in these large gardens was formal. In the dawn of stability after the unrest of the Wars of the Roses, there was a move away from the close confines of the castle. No longer was it necessary to fortify your house with keeps and turrets, moats and drawbridges. In any case, with the invention of gunpowder a means had been found to undermine the strongest castle walls. Following the dissolution of the monasteries and the shift of emphasis from religious to secular building, the manor house became established, and manorial gardens and wildlife blossomed in the new-found liberty of the countryside. But the manors had to be hedged and ditched and it was at this time that topiary came into its own.

One of the earliest accounts of topiary goes back to Roman times when Pliny the Younger's gardeners had perfected the art. It flourished in the grand Italian gardens during Tudor times and was brought back to the Netherlands and Britain in the sixteenth century. Box and yew were the hedging plants mostly used. There are several varieties of box (*Buxus*) and the species most probably in use then was the large green hedging box *Buxus sempervirens*. The second Latin name indicates that it lives for a long time, which indeed it does, being a tough plant native to the chalky areas of Italy, Greece, France, Spain and Britain (as at Box Hill in Surrey). Three other varieties of box are used today: the dwarf edging box, *B.s.* "Suffructicosa", the silver-variegated box *B.s.* "Elegantissima", and the golden box *B. japonica aurea-maculata*.

The closely clipped hedges provided the opportunity to create the knot gardens, mazes and topiary typical of Italian and Tudor gardens such as those of Hever in Kent, ancestral home of Anne Boleyn, Henry VIII's second wife. Formal gardens belonging to royalty might have the king's or queen's beasts neatly carved from the yew, and in informal areas low hedges were used for laying out wet washing for drying in the sun. It is interesting to recall that at this time wooden garden fencing was used and often painted in the owner's heraldic colours. The gaudy colours of today's gardens are just a continuation of this individuality. In England, the gardens at Hever Castle and Hampton Court are some of the finest existing examples of the Tudor period and are open to the public.

The picturesque moated Hever Castle dates back to the thirteenth century. Viscount William Waldorf Astor bought the

A Lady of the Manor supervises a female gardener in this early sixteenth-century Flemish manuscript.

Court with flower beds, sundials and his famous "mount" – a soil mound on a pile of over a quarter of a million bricks, topped by a three-storey building from which could be surveyed the gardens and surrounding countryside. The King could sit there and enjoy the marvellous views and look over his captive "living world". Mounts were a new idea, designed only for royalty or the wealthy with large gardens and sufficient labour and money to construct these considerable piles. It is thought that they may have had their origin in the defensive look-out position of medieval castles built upon a hill. As the need for defence receded, their use became formalized and purely decorative. One still stands within the old city walls of Canterbury in Kent.

Not noted as a naturalist, Henry VIII brought the exciting elements of the chase into his gardens, petrified in stone: dragons, tigers, greyhounds, bulls, harts, badgers, antelopes, griffins, leopards, rams and yales – fabulous horned beasts –

Golden yews have been clipped to form giant chess pieces in the celebrated Chess Garden at Hever Castle, Kent.

PLANTS AND TREES IN TUDOR ENGLAND

The flower beds in Tudor gardens would look fairly familiar in some gardens today.

Much smaller and more informal gardens of family homes contained a riotous collection of pretty flowers including balsam, columbines (aquilegias), gladioli, forget-me-nots, heartsease (*Viola tricolor*), hyacinths, love-in-a-mist (*Nigella damascena*) and old-fashioned roses. The Crusaders had brought back many flowers for the garden, including cyclamens, hollyhocks, jasmine and carnations.

Wild plants of the countryside such as columbines, cowslips and primroses, ordinary daisies, foxgloves and violets were carefully dug up or their seed was collected for sowing, creating a more natural look to the gardens. In England there was great interest in new species brought back from Mediterranean countries where they grew as natives, such as larkspur, delightful with its tall spikes of spurred flowers, the Martagon lily which still grows wild in the forest of the Massif Central, and Madonna lilies (*Lilium candidum*), pansies, peonies (which have naturalized only on Steep Holm in the Bristol Channel), and those old favourites, the *Calendula* pot marigolds.

The most interesting tree of Tudor times is the sycamore (*Acer pseudoplatanus*), first recorded in England in 1579. It is a native of Europe but not of Britain, and may have been established earlier in Scotland, where it is called the plane (not to be confused with London plane, *Platanus x acerifolia*). Sycamore seeds prolifically and has naturalized itself in many suburban and seaside gardens. It is

An ash tree and an almond tree appear in this sixteenth-century English manuscript.

also a nuisance in some wooded habitats such as beech woods, where its seedlings oust the natural assemblage of species and hinder habitat management. In Scotland, sycamore grows especially well and there was an historic specimen at Scone Place, near Perth, reputed to have been planted by Mary Queen of Scots (1542-87). It finally disappeared under a pile of ivy in 1940-1. One village sycamore near Beaminster in Dorset still stands today as the plague tree or posy tree, around which the parishioners would gather with their scented herbs to watch the coffins go off to the mass grave.

Although conservationists may hate sycamore, it is useful as a potential source of food for birds in the garden, particularly attracting aphids. There are over 183 epiphytes (organisms like lichens which live on the bark) and parasites recorded from sycamore.

At least two fine oaks are associated with Queen Elizabeth I, one ivy-clad stump in Greenwich Park – once a royal residence – and another on the green of Northiam in Kent, under which she is said to have changed her shoes! These English oaks are the common or pedunculate (acorns with stalks) oaks, *Quercus robur*. Oaks in any garden are a bonus since they harbour more forms of wild life than any other tree in Britain: over 300 species of insect have been recorded from the English oak. There are 66 other species of oak in Britain, most of them introduced, but they have fewer associated insect species. It has now been proved that the longer a tree has been established as a native, the more insect species there are associated with it. The Chilean monkey-puzzle tree (*Araucaria araucana*) for instance, introduced to England in the last century, sponsors few, if any, insects.

Ever since medieval days the black poplar (*Populus nigra*) of the English countryside had been eagerly sought after by craftsmen needing cruck beams for their timber-framed buildings and they were still valued in Tudor times. Today black poplars have become extinct in some counties. They are particularly attractive and would be a good species to plant in the garden to help their conservation. White poplars (*P. alba*) were frequently planted in Tudor gardens for the attractive white underside of the leaves and the white bark scattered with black diamond marks. White and grey poplars are still popular trees in gardens today.

Purple hairstreak butterfly
(*Quercusia quercus*)

ON THE OAK

Oaks harbour a rich variety of wildlife, especially beetles and moth caterpillars which defoliate the trees, or sit camouflaged on the bark. The gnarled trunks and hollowed interiors of thc Tudor oaks also provided a refuge for birds and bats.

Oak hook-tip moth
(*Drepana binaria*)

Longhorned moth
(*Nemophora degeerella*)

Oak lutestring moth
(*Cymatophorima diluta*)

Scalloped oak moth
(*Crocallis elinguaria*)

**Green
oak tortrix moth**
(*Tortrix viridana*)

**Pale brindled
beauty caterpillar**
(*Apocheima pilosaria*)

Stag beetle
(*Lucanus cervus*)

Cockchafer
(*Melolontha melolontha*)

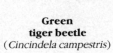

**Green
tiger beetle**
(*Cincindela campestris*)

Green shield bug
(*Palomena prasina*)

V.B.

dilapidated property in 1903 and the recreated Tudor garden seen today is the work of some 1,000 workmen who toiled for four years. Among the reinstated Tudor features are rose gardens, a croquet lawn, a maze and, unique to Hever, a chess garden, where clipped golden yew has been used for the set pieces. There are the usual arbours of jasmine, clematis and honeysuckle.

PHYSIC AND BOTANIC GARDENS

The first physic garden in western Europe was established in Tudor times and had its origins in the fine formal gardens of northern Italy. The philosophy and natural sciences of the learned developed with the cultivation of medicinal or "physic" plants for physicians. The garden at Pisa was established first, it is thought, in 1543 supplying medicinal plants for research and for use. Within two years, others were opened in Italy, at Padua and in Florence.

This was a time of great exploration and discovery of new plants; botanists, as naturalists, were learning more about the virtues of plants grown especially for man, and at the same time many strange and exotic plants brought to Europe by the travellers and explorers of the age were established in botanic gardens in the centres of learning and education. These gardens soon became commonplace in Europe and over the next century botanic and physic gardens served the universities in Bologna, Edinburgh, Leyden, Montpellier and Oxford; the famous Chelsea Physic Garden was not established until late in the Jacobean period in 1673 by the Worshipful Society of Apothecaries of London.

Many interesting species of plants made their way to the botanic gardens and undoubtedly into some private gardens at this time. For instance, crown imperial fritillaries from Turkey and Persia were seen for the first time in Europe in the 1570s; potatoes arrived in England in the 1580s, tomatoes and tobacco a little earlier – all from America; the French marigold (*Tagetes patula*) towards the end of the century, and the *Hyacinthus romanus* came through southern France from North Africa in about 1596.

An important botanist of the sixteenth century, Charles de L'Ecluse, also known as Carolus Clusius (1526-1609), a Frenchman of Flemish ancestry, was responsible for introducing tulips and the horse chestnut to Europe from Greece while he was in Vienna. He became the director of the botanic garden at Leyden in 1593, and is sometimes referred

to as the Father of Scientific Botany. At the time of his appointment he was a frail old man. He had been trained in medicine at Montpellier in southern France, and had spent his life travelling as a keen botanist, describing 200 new species from Spain and Portugal in 1564-5, setting up a *Hortus Medicus* (medicinal garden) in Vienna in 1573 for Emperor Maximillian II, and collecting in Austria, Hungary and Germany.

Clusius worked with Dirk Cluyt, who also latinised his name to Clutius (the standard joke was Clusius and Clutius), and in 1594 planted up the botanic garden at Leyden with about 1,000 species of plants. Though no longer in existence today, the garden was recreated in 1931 by Professor Baus Becking. L'Ecluse also translated old Dutch and Italian herbals and Garcia di Orta's Portuguese book on Indian plants into Latin.

Other scientists of the period who also contributed to botanical literature were Leonhardt Fuchs (1501-66) and Rembert Dodoens (1517-85). There was also Konrad von Gesner (1516-65), who wrote *Historia plantarum*, but after his death the manuscript was lost and it was 1751 before it was found and finally published.

It was during the Tudor period that some of the first English books on gardening came to be written with the publication by the herbalist William Turner, known as "the father of English botany", of his treatise on plant names in 1548, followed in 1558 by an unoriginal but practical gardening book by Thomas Hill, culled mainly from Continental sources.

CHAPTER THREE

PATTERNS
OF
PLEASURE
(1550 – 1600)

Plants continued to arrive in Europe from all over the world and keen gardener-naturalists experimented with growing all sorts of new and exotic species. It was during this period that tobacco and potatoes were introduced from the New World.

The first true gardening books appeared around the middle of the sixteenth century. More botanic gardens were established in or around major centres of learning and the study of botany progressed greatly. The first useful books on identifying birds were published during this period, too. An increased awareness of, and growing interest in, plants and wildlife is reflected in much of the contemporary literature – given additional impetus in England by a vogue for "horti-cultural" poems dedicated to Elizabeth I, the "flowery" queen. Shakespeare, an enthusiastic amateur naturalist, mentions over 60 different species of birds in his writings and he makes many delightful allusions to different cultivated and wild flowers.

The gardens at Hatfield House, Hertfordshire, feature many Elizabethan plants.

Modern Elizabethan-style gardens are a delight to see, but for all their beauty, they are based on only a few contemporary descriptions of the originals. We do know, however, that these gardens were lavishly designed around fine manor houses.

During Elizabeth's reign, several great houses and gardens were built or enlarged, houses such as Hardwick Hall in Derbyshire, Burghley, Holdenby and Kirby Hall (all in Northamptonshire), Longleat in Wiltshire and Sissinghurst in Kent. Wollaton Hall in Nottinghamshire was another; this was later the home of Sir Francis Willughby, whose son was to become patron of the naturalist John Ray in the seventeenth century. Another important house and garden which was built in 1570 was Kelmscott Manor. The designer William Morris stayed at Kelmscott 200 years later, and was enchanted with the old garden and adjacent water meadows. Perhaps it was the beauty of places such as this that inspired him to create his superb range of furnishings with "natural" floral designs.

Many of the noble families of the Elizabethan period had to be prepared to entertain the Queen and her huge entourage as she made her annual progress round the country, staying in the houses of her subjects on the way. Often this led to extensive rebuilding and reconstruction: the estates had to be large enough to provide meat for all the guests, who might well number over 50 people, and the gardens able to supply sufficient vegetables and fruit for the table. The owners went to great lengths to please their monarch. At least one house, Holdenby, was specially built for the purpose, and in *Floraes Paradise* (1608) Sir Hugh Platt describes how at Beddington Sir Francis Carew successfully retarded the ripening of a cherry tree to coincide with the Queen's visit, the fruit of which ". . . he had of purpose kept back from ripening at least one month after all cherries had taken their farewell of England: he had done this by putting on a canvas cover and keeping it damp . . ."

THE ELIZABETHAN GARDEN

By Elizabeth's reign it had become fashionable for the manor estates and gardens of the wealthy to be sited at the top of a hill overlooking parkland or rolling countryside. The gardens were nearly always aligned east-west to take full advantage of the warmth of the southerly sun. The technique of raising water from rivers, sinking wells, storing and channelling it to fountains and grottoes had been known before Tudor times in England; the art of raising water went back in history to classical Greece and Rome, and to the Egyptians on the banks of the Nile. Already the use of water had reached a high point of sophistication in Renaissance Europe, and the joke fountain was very popular. Hidden pipes and sources of water would be turned on from a concealed tap to drench the unsuspecting visitor. Lead cisterns were used to store water for watering plants, raising fish, and even for bathing in; canals were built suitable for small boats from which to appreciate the scents and sights of herb gardens, knots and arbours.

The Elizabethan love of intricacy can be seen in the convoluted pattern of the ornamental knot garden. Usually geometric in design, the edging would be carried out in scented herbs such as lavender, thrift, cotton lavender or thyme; sometimes rosemary or box. The centre of the pattern might be filled with flowers, herbs or perhaps just gravel, sand or brick dust in pleasing colours. Similarly the maze was a popular feature of the Elizabethan garden, with its appeal of puzzlement, and was to be found in most of the big gardens of the sixteenth century. In England these mazes may have had their origin in the "labyrinths" of the early church, originally marked out in stone or tiles or cut into the turf outside the church for the penitent to follow as a further exercise towards spiritual perfection. The ornamental maze of Renaissance Europe, however, seems to have sprung into fashion through the belief that it was a legacy of Roman style.

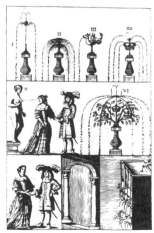

Left: A lever-action pump in use in a late sixteenth-century garden.

Right: Recreated at the Stoke Flower festival, a Tudor knot garden demonstrates the typical box borders enclosing culinary herbs. Growing vegetables like this was in the style of a potager. Stone mini-beasts set off these private gardens. Only royalty and the aristocracy had these semi-formal gardens at this time.

Above: In the Elizabethan period geometrically designed beds in intricate patterns displayed edible and medicinal plants. Fountains were much in evidence. The new gardens at the 15th-century Old Palace at Hatfield are planted with a maze of box and plants introduced in the 15th, 16th and 17th centuries.

Left: These designs for joke fountains were drawn in 1677.

There was nothing secretive about them as there was later in the man-high hedges of Hampton Court, created in 1699; the Elizabethan mazes were often only a foot or two high, built of box or yew, hyssop, cotton lavender or thyme, and designed for the pleasure of viewing and enjoying the scent of the plants.

About the middle of the century the first true gardening books began to appear. The *Hundred Good Pointes of Husbandrie*, by Thomas Tusser, was published in 1557. This was a mixture of good advice for the farmer and gardener, offered in gentle rhyming couplets:

In Feverall rest not for taking thine ease:
get into the grounde with thy beans and thy peas.

For flax and for hemp, for to have of her owne:
the wife must in May take good hede it be sowne.

This work is of particular interest for the wide variety of plants recommended and listed under their various headings: for example, "Herbs and roots for sallets and sauce" (twenty-one of them); "seeds and herbs for the kitchen" (forty-three are listed); nine "herbs and roots to boil or to butter". It ran into twelve editions, an indication of the upsurge of interest in the practical aspect of horticulture and the growing market for information on all matters of cultivation.

Thomas Hill's *Most Briefe and Pleasaunte Treatise* appeared in 1558. Like its French counterpart *Praedium Rusticum*, by Charles Estienne (1554), it drew largely on Continental material already published, but the author's later works, the *Proffitable Arte of Gardening* (1568) and *Gardener's Labyrinth* (1577), fully illustrated with woodcuts, were of better practical use, being more obviously based on the author's own experience and containing much sound gardening advice:

"The placing of a garden-ground near to a Fenne or Marrish (marsh), is everie where to be misliked and refused for the ayre thereabouts doth ingender either the Pestilence, or wicked vermin, much harming the garden-plot lying nigh to it."

The techniques of printing and quality of reproduction had advanced considerably and from sources such as these and the embroidery and tapestries that have survived in England and on the Continent, we can assume a fair picture of what

Above: The title page of Thomas Hill's Most Briefe and Pleasaunte Treatise *(c. 1558).*

Left: This early seventeenth-century style mount in the Queen's Garden at Kew Palace, Richmond, Surrey, was constructed in the 1960s.

Above: A seventeenth-century design for a decorative lattice work screen.

Below: A section of the parterre at Herrenhausen, Hanover.

the gardens of the larger houses must have looked like during the latter half of the sixteenth century.

The typical Elizabethan garden still retained the traditional rectangular shape and was divided into sections of equal proportions. These would be for vegetables, herbs and fruit; a knot garden, probably a maze, and in one or more corners there would be a mount, still an important feature from which the owner could look out over the outer boundary. This might consist of a wooden palisade or a hedge of quickthorn. Sometimes there would be heraldic figures and lattice work, carved by carpenters and often brightly painted, with arbours supporting climbing plants such as honeysuckles and vines. Fantastic topiary with the figures of men and beasts were also popular features of the period.

Writing in 1599, a Swiss visitor to England, Thomas Platter, describes his impressions after visiting Hampton Court:

"... There was a fine large fountain wrought of white marble, with an excellent water work with which one may easily spray any ladies or others standing about, and wet them well.

"I noticed numerous patches where square cavities had been scooped, as for paving stones; some of these were filled with red brick-dust, some with white sand, and some with green lawn, very much resembling a chess-board. The hedges and surrounds were of hawthorn, bush firs, ivy, roses, juniper, holly, English or common elm, box and other shrubs, very gay and attractive.

"There were all manner of shapes, men and women, half men and half horse, sirens, serving-maids with baskets, French lilies and delicate crenellations all round made from dry twigs bound together and the aforesaid evergreen quickset shrubs, or entirely of rosemary, all true to the life, and so cleverly and amusingly interwoven, mingled and grown together, trimmed and arranged picture-wise, that their equal would be difficult to find."

These were the best Elizabethan gardens in England. Little information exists as to the nature of the cottage gardens of the period. Herbs would, of course, have been grown in all sorts of gardens from the grandest to the poorest. Colourful and aromatic herb gardens contained germander, speedwell (*Veronica chamaedrys*), lovage, rue, sage and thyme. Wildlife would have thrived in the neat parcels of gardens separated by clipped hedges; dragonflies and damselflies would have danced over the ponds.

This was an age of exploration: new plant species were being brought in from all over the world. As trade flourished and colonization took place overseas, the long reign of Elizabeth brought stability and cultural advancement. Scientific knowledge was expanding rapidly, not least in the field of natural history, with improved means of communication and the consequent spread of ideas.

THE
EARLY NATURALISTS

The most important British naturalist of the period was William Turner (ca. 1508-68), whose writings justifiably earned him the title of 'father of English botany'. He was given this grand title for his outstanding contribution to the early study of plants, and especially for his celebrated *New Herbal*, published in a series of parts in 1551, 1562 and 1568.

After studying at Cambridge in 1526 Turner had to leave England because of his religious views. This gave him the opportunity of travelling through Europe, where he studied medicine and saw for the first time some of the wild flowers of France, Germany, Italy and Switzerland. His herbarium collection is one of the earliest surviving in England. On his eventual return he became physician to the Lord Protector, Edward Seymour, Duke of Somerset (1506-52) at his new country house at Syon, built between 1520 and 1598. (A "country house" was the term for a grand mansion; a "residence" described the houses of ordinary gentlefolk; and there were rural cottages for commoners.) The Syon house and park-like gardens set around a lake remain little changed to this day, where they now lie under the flight path to Heathrow Airport and are open to the public. The gardens contain a remarkable collection of mature trees and indeed there must have been a unique collection then. Referring for instance to the pomegranate, Turner remarks that "there are certain in my Lord's garden at Syon, but their fruit cometh never to perfection".

Turner became Dean of Wells Cathedral in Somerset in 1551, soon after the first part of the *New Herbal* was published. The first mention in England of jasmine, winter cherry or Chinese lantern (*Physalis alkekengi*) and French marigold (*Tagetes patula*), "the velvet flower or French marigold", can be found in the *New Herbal*; French marigolds had arrived from Mexico, perhaps by way of France. Garden snapdragons (*Antirrhinum majus*) came from Italy and were delightfully referred to as "broad calf's snout".

Turner was the first to record the native dog's mercury (*Mercurialis perennis* – supposedly poisonous to dogs) growing in the woods around London. *The Times* newspaper recently devoted a column to its usefulness as one of the hundred or more "indicator plants" – their presence in a beech wood indicates an ancient habitat several hundred years old.

Probably the greatest influence on contemporary botanical thought was that of the botanist Charles de L'Ecluse, known as Clusius (1526-1609). Internationally famous, he

Matthias de L'Obel (1538-1616) botanist and physician to King James I.
Below: *A monstrous whale from Edward Topsell's* Historie of Serpents *(1608). Topsell's book was much influenced by Gesner's* Historia Animalium *(1551-87).*

visited England on at least two occasions in 1571 and 1581 and knew many of the influential people of the day. His *Rariorum Plantarum Historia*, published in 1601, was a classic work.

The English contribution to the natural history of the time tended to be supportive rather than innovative. When the French botanist Matthias de L'Obel came to England shortly after 1584 his patron was Baron Zouche, whose interest in horticulture led him to build Bramshill in Hampshire and a garden at Hackney which was renowned for its imported plants. While supervising his patron's garden at Hackney, L'Obel prepared a catalogue of British flora and kept in touch with many of the eminent botanists of the day. He had travelled extensively in Europe collecting plants and was a competent author. He described the succulent yucca and raised the medicinal thorn apple (*Datura stramonium*), both from America, the dog's tooth violet (*Erythronium dens-canis*), an ornamental vine, and other plants imported by Lord Zouche. L'Obel's work was honoured by Linnaeus two centuries later when he gave his name to the genus *Lobelia*.

Meanwhile on the Continent, another learned physician and lover of flowers, Konrad von Gesner (1516-65), a Swiss-German often called the "German Pliny", wrote two books on plants, *Historia Plantarum* (1541) and *Catalogus plantarum* (1542), though the manuscript of the first was mislaid and was not published until 1751. Von Gesner loved the mountains for their colourful alpines (a coveted specialist group in today's gardens), and vowed to climb a different peak each year, but he eventually died of the plague. Among his books on animals, his *Historia Animalium* (1551-87) stands as the foundation of modern zoology.

Naturalists and physicians freely moved plants around the world.
Top left: *The Chinese lantern* (Physalis alkekengi) *came from China.*

Top right: *Snapdragons* (Antirrhinum majus) *came from the Mediterranean.*

Bottom left: *The emetic, laxative and purgative dog's mercury* (Mercurialis perennis) *from Europe was soon naturalized in America.*

Bottom right: *The thorn apple* (Datura stramonium) *was brought to Europe from America.*

INTREPID COLLECTORS

Gardening in Elizabeth's reign continued to be influenced by the introductions of plants from Europe, the Far East and from North and South America, where many of her subjects went in search of new sea routes or followed the lure of El Dorado's treasure. Some of these plant hunters sent their findings to the physic garden in Holborn of John Gerard (1545-1612), or to Theobalds, home of William Cecil, Lord Burleigh, where Gerard was his gardener. Gerard had his own collectors in the South of France sending back new species and varieties of roses, viburnums, daphnes, cistuses and prickly pear (*Opuntia microdasys rufida*), originally from South America; other plants were sent from the Continent to Gerard's patron. Native honeysuckles, clematis and hibiscus (*Hibiscus syriacus*) came in from places as far apart as Switzerland and Syria.

In about 1578 tulips first arrived in England for Gerard by a secret route from Vienna. Through the centuries good money has always been paid for interesting or rare plants. That Gerard had few scruples about his sources was only too apparent when he published his famous *Herball* in 1597, most of which had been "borrowed" from the work of the Belgian botanist Rembert Dodoens. In the previous year Gerard had brought out his *Catalogue*, consisting of a list of over a thousand plants grown in his own garden, many of them new introductions. With the sponsorship of Burleigh and a preface by L'Obel himself, Gerard's *Catalogue* was assured of acceptance, and the *Herball* proved a best seller.

There were other sources of plants in Europe for Gerard and William Cecil. From France the naturalist-gardener, Jean Robin (1550-1629), who looked after the *Jardin des Plantes* in Paris, sent Gerard barrenwort (*Epimedium alpinum*), a herbal plant supposedly endowed with the powers of inducing fertility in barren women. Robin's son Vespasien (1579-1662) also became a celebrated botanist. Solomon's seal (*Polygonatum multiflorum*), now a common garden plant, was sent by the energetic Clusius from Leyden. According to the chronicler of botanical history, John Claudius Loudon (1783-1843), some 200 years later, at least 84 plant species were introduced to England in the sixteenth century, and many of these might have been found in Gerard's garden at Holborn.

In his *Herball*, John Gerard is illustrated holding the flowers and fruit of the potato, and states that the plant came from Virginia. This is very odd since the potato is not a native of Eastern America. It comes from the Andes in South America, growing at a height of between 2 to 3,800m (6,600 to 12,789 ft). Archaeological evidence, backed up with radiocarbon dating (a scientific test to calculate the geological age of an organism), indicates that the potato was cultivated in Peru, presumably in small gardens, as early as 8,000 years ago. There are 200 wild species of potato and it remains the most cultivated crop in the world.

Hibiscuses belong to the mallow family and grow in the tropics and sub-tropics. Some 300 species are found in China, Syria, Africa and south-eastern America. Favoured as a beautiful greenhouse plant, the large flowers of hibiscus unfurl to reveal a long floral arm. At the base of the petals are nectaries whose sugary nectar is very attractive to butterflies.

It is quite probable that Gerard, who is credited with the earliest mention of the potato in any European book, received it from Sir Francis Drake, who sailed back to England in 1586 from North America with some of the settlers, including the mathematician Thomas Harriot (1560-1621). Harriot may also have obtained the tubers on behalf of his patron Raleigh.

Whilst both Raleigh and Drake were overseas exploring, they were also sacking Spanish ports and rifling galleons of supplies. Livestock, fruit and vegetables were seized at every opportunity and it may have been through this route that the potato reached Britain, for it is known that Spanish galleons were often stocked with potatoes at this time.

The plant was probably first introduced to Europe through Spain as it appears in a list of Seville hospital's provisions for 1573, indicating that the tubers had been grown locally. They may have been brought over from South America in the 1560s.

Io: Payne ſculp.

Left: *The title page of the third edition of John Gerard's Herball (1636). John Gerard is illustrated beneath the title.*

Below: *Solomon's seal, from Gerard's Herball.*

The astute and learned botanist Clusius from Leyden Physic Garden mentioned in his *Historia Plantarum* (1601) that he had seen the potato as early as 1588. It remained a botanical curiosity until the mid-eighteenth century.

The history of Ireland is inextricably tied up with the potato and it is highly likely that Raleigh introduced it around Cork and Waterford in the south when he took possession of the extensive lands granted to him. Little could he have realized that the introduction of the potato was such a milestone in Irish history, let alone in gardening. The lazy beds of long-forgotten potato patches still mark the Irish countryside, and recall the famine of 1846, 300 years later, when blight destroyed the entire crop.

Sir Walter Raleigh is also credited with the introduction of tobacco to England. It had been used by the North American Indians and was thought to have medicinal powers. Such an interesting plant was soon shipped back to Europe as a novelty. Today it is only grown as a crop in Europe in a small way in the warmest parts of the south. It was originally introduced to France in 1556, Portugal in 1558, Spain the following year and England in 1565. Tobacco was given its generic name of *Nicotiana* after Jean Nicot, the French Ambassador to Lisbon, who, it is said, presented Catherine de' Medici with some seeds. In America, tobacco was destined to make the settlers in Virginia and Maryland rich enough to develop some fine European-looking gardens of their own.

Many other plants were being exchanged throughout Europe. In the middle of Elizabeth's reign the Dean of Windsor, William Harrison (1534-93), noted that all sorts of fruits and strange herbs were coming in daily "from the

Left: *Planting out orange trees in the seventeenth century, from* Spring *by David Teniers the Younger (c. 1644).*

Indies, Americas, Taprobane (Ceylon), Canary Isles and all parts of the world . . . I have seen capers, oranges and lemons, and heard of wild olives growing here, besides other strange trees brought here from afar, whose names I know not". There was a great quest to discover new species and many attempts were made to grow exotic plants in British gardens. It is believed that Sir Walter Raleigh was responsible for introducing the orange tree to Britain, presenting some pips to his kinsman Sir Francis Carew (of cherry-tree fame) who had filled his new garden at Beddington with imported fruit trees. Others have it that the plants were imported direct from Italy. The orange trees, planted in the open ground, were protected in winter by a "wooden tabernacle" as the diarist John Evelyn described it in 1658, and heated by stoves.

Above: *Working in a walled orchard, from William Lawson's* A New Orchard and Garden *(1618).*

Below: *A native of the Mediterranean, the caper* (Capparis spinosa) *has a tough stem with spines and a straggling form. It is the unopened flower buds which are picked and pickled for the table.*

THE COTTAGE GARDEN

By the latter part of the sixteenth century the cottage garden was coming into its own. Many garden plants, discarded from the great gardens, had found their way there to augment the herbs and medicinal plants so necessary to good husbandry. Something of the nature of these gardens can be gleaned from the writings of the poets of the day. Describing a garden in 1563, the poet and botanist Dr John Hall wrote:

It hedged was with honeysuckles
Or periclimenum;
Well mixed with small cornus trees (dogwood),
Sweet briar and ligustrum (wild rose and privet).

The white thorn, and the blackthorn both,
With box, and maple fine:
In which branched the briony,
The ivy and wild vine.

The wildlife that Shakespeare (1564-1616) was accustomed to as a boy enriched his writings. He was an amateur naturalist who knew his wild flowers, garden flowers and birds better than most. The sights and sounds of the English countryside – of rooks, plovers and skylarks – were part of the substance of his plays and poetry. Shakespeare loved his garden, especially his trees, flowers and birds.

BIRDS IN THE GARDEN

esearchers have recorded 60 species of bird mentioned in Shakespeare's writings. Most people would have difficulty recording the same number around their own house and garden today; it is clear that he was a competent amateur ornithologist.

There were thought to have been only 150 species of bird known in Britain in Elizabethan times. The first useful books on identifying birds were published about the middle of the sixteenth century, among them *Avium Praeciparum* (1544) by William Turner, the author of the *New Herbal*. Before that there had been nothing of significance since medieval days when the

remarkable German Emperor Frederick II (1194-1250), a born naturalist, had written the first illustrated bird book, *De arte venande cum avibus (The art of hunting with birds)*, which covered a wider field than the title suggests.

The French naturalist Pierre Belon (1517-64), a doctor, produced a work on the nature of birds in the middle of the century but, like Gesner, his studies of animals were a curious mixture of fact and legend. He did, however, establish that a bat was a mammal, and not a bird.

Dovecots were commonplace in sixteenth century gardens, not just for the pleasure of seeing doves fluttering down to

pick up grain but to keep a supply of birds for the table. There were probably more people catching wild birds for food in the country or in the garden than admiring them. Small birds were caught with "lime" – a sticky concoction of lime and water pasted on to posts and walls in which the bird's feet stuck fast – and hawking for herons was an everyday event. Herons were easy targets for swift-flying hawks and were regarded as a nuisance, as often they are today, eating fish from lakes and fishponds. Thrushes and other song birds were caged and kept in gardens, having been reared from eggs collected from the nest. It was still not known where migratory birds went to in winter.

Skylark
(*Alauda arvensis*)

Red kite
(*Milvus milvus*)

Great crested grebe
(*Podiceps cristatus*)

Raven
(*Corvus corax*)

Chough
(*Pyrrhocorax pyrrhocorax*)

A nobleman courting a young lady, from a sixteenth-century Flemish manuscript. Nesting storks and a hawk look on.

Many of the plants to which Shakespeare refers in his plays – lady's smock (*Cardamine pratensis*), the woodbine (honeysuckle, *Lonicera* spp.), eglantine (sweet briar, *Rosa canina*), oxslips, wild thyme, violets, rosemary, musk roses, wormwood (*Artemisia absinthium*) and yew – are wild species of the countryside, especially the herbs which thrive on the chalky Chilterns and Downs. They would have been grown in gardens for their colours, scent and symbolism. Shakespeare's works are full of delightful allusions:

"There's rosemary, that's for remembrance:
Pray you, love, remember: and there is pansies,
That's for thoughts.
There's fennel for you, and columbines:
There's rue for you; and here's some for me . . ."
(*Hamlet*, Act IV, Scene 5)

NAMES TO REMEMBER

Botanical natural history was making great strides in Europe and there were plenty of professional botanists, physicians and amateur naturalists keenly pursuing the subject. Wild plants of distant continents were being raised as garden plants in another country with a strange climate. But the naturalist-botanists whose names are honoured retrospectively in today's plant names tended to be the famous who had their own gardens or looked after the gardens of their patrons. Details of ordinary Elizabethans and their cottage gardens have been lost in antiquity.

One such person whose name is recalled in the genus *Robinia*, which includes widely grown species of ornamental tree, is Jean Robin (1550-1629), the gardener and herbalist to Henri IV and Louis XIII of France, and Director of the *Jardin des Plantes* in Paris. The false acacia or locust tree (*Robinia pseudoacacia*) is widespread on riverbeds and roadsides through much of the Continent, but it is a native of the Appalachians in North America from Pennsylvania southwards, and was in cultivation in both France and England by the 1630s, perhaps earlier. It has great tolerance to a polluted atmosphere, and is a useful tree in city parks and gardens.

Two Spanish botanists who made notes about some of the new plants being brought back on Spanish galleons from the Americas are remembered in plant names. Monardas, lively herbaceous border plants with their showy red flowers, recall the doctor-botanist Nicholas Monardes (1493-1588), and lopezias commemorate Thomas Lopez (ca. 1540). One favourite plant in the garden, honeysuckle (*Lonicera*), is named after another botanist of the sixteenth century, the German Adam Lonitzer (1528-86). So close was the study of botany to medicine that plants were often named after physicians.

Two other important sixteenth-century botanists were Pierandrea Matthioli (1500-77) in Italy who gave his name to stocks, *Matthiola*, and L'Obel, after whom Linnaeus named *Lobelia* in the eighteenth century. One of our present-day woodland flowers, *Cortusa*, was named after Jacobi Antonia Cortusi (1513-93), the Director of Padua, one of the earliest physic gardens established in this Elizabethan period.

LATE SIXTEENTH-CENTURY PLANT INTRODUCTIONS TO ENGLAND

Aloe barbadensis 1596

Barren-wort
(*Epimedium alpinum*) 1597

Globe thistle
(*Echinops ritro*) 1570

Geranium dalmaticum 1576

Goat's rue
(*Galega officinalis*) 1568

Hairy spurge
(*Euphorbia pilosa*) 1576

Honesty (*Lunaria annua*) 1570

Holm oak (*Quercus ilex*) 1580

Love-lies-bleeding
(*Amaranthus caudatus*) 1596

Mallow-leaved convolulus
(*Convolvulus* spp.) 1597

Love-lies-bleeding

Marigold
(*Calendula officinalis*) 1578

Oleander
(*Nerium oleander*) 1596

Spotted yellow lily
(*Lilium pyrenaicum*) 1596

Thorn apple (*Datura stramonium*)
Late sixteenth century

Valerian (*Valeriana officinalis*)
Late sixteenth century

Wallflower
(*Cheiranthus cheiri*) 1573

Winter aconite
(*Eranthis hyemalis*) 1596

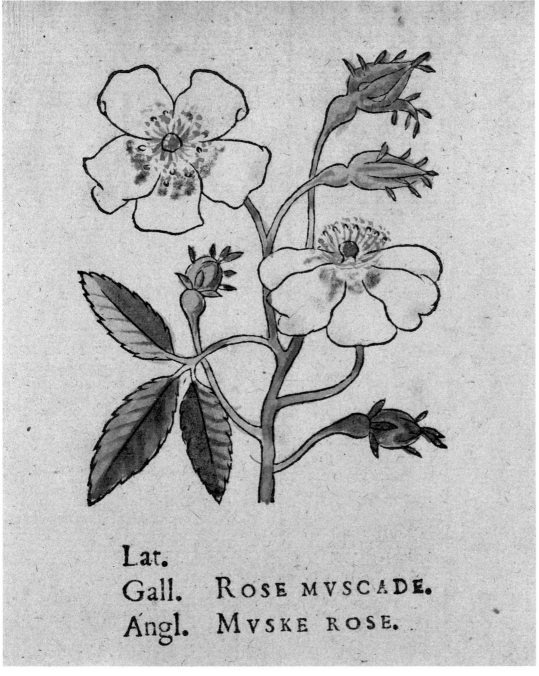

Lat.
Gall. ROSE MVSCADE.
Angl. MVSKE ROSE.

Left: *The musk rose, from* La clef des champs *by Jacques le Moyne de Morgues (1586). John Gerard described the "Muske Rose" as having very sharp prickles "long leaves smooth and shining" and flowers "of a white colour".*

Below: *Garlic, from Matthioli's* Commentarii *(1565).*

Right: *Lady's smock (Cardamine pratensis) is an attractive wayside plant in Europe with relatives in America and Asia.*

Left: *The pink acacia (Robinia hispida) was named by Carl Linnaeus after Jean Robin, who first grew this tree in Europe. It is a native of south-eastern America.*

MEDICINAL PLANTS

There is much controversy about whether the first physic garden was established in Pisa or Padua, but it is thought likely that the Pisa garden was already in existence before the Padua garden was officially founded by the Venetian Senate (137 for, 3 against and 17 don't knows) on 29th May 1545. The Pisa garden was sited on old royal gardens which included ornamental and herbal gardens and had a distinct botanical leaning. Even 100 years earlier a Parco Reale had been planted by Alfonso II of Aragon between 1450-70, so it had ancient origins. Typical Mediterranean plants were grown in this park including olives, citrus fruits, pomegranates and figs.

The physic garden at Florence was also established in 1545 and the *Jardin de Botanique de l'école de Médécin* in Montpellier (southern France) was founded in 1598 in the centre of the town.

Some physic gardens, like the *Jardin des Plantes* in Paris founded in 1593 by Henry IV of France (1553-1610), were set up with royal backing. They were usually situated in university cities where serious academic study could be carried out on plants. Montpellier, for instance, offered a place where physicians, who were not encouraged to practise in Paris, could carry out their studies.

The original purpose of most physic gardens was to supply fresh medicinal herbs to physicians to fight the many scourges of the time. Today their role has changed completely. They specialize in representing as many different plants (mostly non-medicinal) from as many different countries as possible. Small collections of medicinal plants are still kept to remind students of the traditional past and the continued dependence on a severely limited number of drug plants used today.

Britain was late in establishing a physic garden: Oxford was not founded until 1621 and Chelsea Physic Garden was established in 1673.

Many of the plants newly introduced during the sixteenth century were highly valued for their medicinal use. From South Africa to Europe, through the trading routes with Barbados in the West Indies, came the *Aloe* plants, whose extracts were much used as a purgative and tonic. *Aloe barbadensis* was imported to England from 1596 onwards and grown in gardens for its medicinal use. The plants had been known since the first century AD, since they appeared in one of Dioscorides's lists (Chapter 1, page 16).

An important medicinal plant cultivated in London at least from the end of the sixteenth century was the thorn apple (*Datura stramonium*) which had been described earlier by L'Obel. In Virginia it was also known as the Devil's apple, Jamestownweed or Jimsonweed since early colonists arriving in Virginia had sampled it thinking it was a form of spinach. They went mad and almost died from the effects. Unknown to the colonists the plant, which is a

The Physic Garden at Padua. The plants have changed since the sixteenth century but the garden layout remains the same.

A physic garden of 1500. Herbs were grown here and their essential oils and essences were distilled in the alembic ovens illustrated.

member of the nightshade family (*Solanaceae*), contains powerful toxins which act as narcotics. The poisonous seeds were used covertly by thieves and prostitutes who wanted to subdue their subjects before robbery. Jimsonweed had its medicinal virtues, however, and was brought to Europe. Smoking the large leaves gave some relief to the nasal passages and the fumes were found to be good for treating asthma and coughs. It became abundant on disturbed ground in London in the eighteenth century, but today the plant is sadly an infrequent species in the countryside and hardly ever grown in the garden, despite its magnificent appearance.

The apple-like fruits are poisonous, and a danger to children.

Another important addition to the Elizabethan garden was valerian (*Valeriana officinalis*), a native of Britain and Europe which is credited with many medicinal qualities. In medieval times it was called "all heal" – not to be confused with comfrey (*Symphytum officinale*) the "cure-all", or with self-heal (*Prunella vulgaris*). From its roots was extracted an oil containing alkaloids which was used as a sedative and anti-spasmodic, especially against epilepsy. Sometimes this valuable oil was adulterated with marsh valerian (*Valeriana dioica*).

HERBS AND THEIR MEANINGS

Herbal medicine was regularly practised in the Elizabethan age, just as in medieval times – the same diseases were still rife and the herb garden was the only source of valuable medicines. The grand physic gardens grew plants for the physicians who treated the well-to-do but ordinary people had to rely on what they could grow themselves, or were collected by the local "wise women". There were plenty of wild plants for people to choose from: in England at least the average number of plant species per parish is about 400-500, and these would have been augmented by introduced species with proven medicinal qualities.

Though many people put their faith in this form of healing most of the concoctions were formulated without any scientific basis. Several of the commoner wild plants such as heartsease violets, coltsfoot (*Tussilago farfara*) and feverfew (*Chrysanthemum parthenium*) were collected from the countryside; others were specially grown close to the house, along with rarer and more coveted species, such as birthwort, monkshood and henbane.

However bizarre the treatment, these herbal remedies were passed down from generation to generation and carefully assessed through trial and error. By chance herbalists did stumble upon some good cures which later proved to be soundly based.

It was firmly believed that God put various plants on earth expressly for man's use. If a plant looked like a part of the body, inside or out, then it provided the necessary "signature" for its use on man. Red plants, like elder and centaury, symbolizing the

colour of blood, were called bloodworts or woundworts and they were used for many problems associated with blood flow. It was this tradition that provided the basis for Nicholas Culpeper's Doctrine of Signatures, which he postulated in his *English Physician* published in the following century, in 1653.

Great emphasis was put on plants which could stop blood flowing or heal bruised muscles. There must have been plenty of serious cuts and lacerations from working in the fields with vicious hooks, scythes and sickles. Duels and bloody battles were all too frequent and treating casualties must have stretched local herbalists to their limits. At least ten completely different plants were given the term bloodwort, from

Above: A Persian herbalist, from a fifteenth-century engraving.

Below: Alembic ovens, from Matthioli's Commentarii. They were used to convert herbs into medical potions.

common centaury (*Centaurium erythraea*) to herb Robert (*Geranium robertianum*), and from the red-veined wood dock (*Rumex sanguineus*) to elder (*Sambucus nigra*), whose ripe fruits ooze a red juice.

There were staunchworts, stabworts and staggerworts, too, for treating "the staggers" in cattle, where the animal literally staggers about. The condition still afflicts farm animals today, but the Elizabethans were hardly to know that it is caused by a dietary deficiency of magnesium.

The most important signature was there for all to see in St John's wort (*Hypericum perforatum*). Its small leaves have tiny perforations like the holes in the body through which blood would flow, and an infusion of the leaves and flowers in vegetable oil turns the oil blood red – a surprising but highly significant sign likely to reassure any doubters. Another signature was seen in birthwort (*Aristolochia clematitis*), a Mediterranean plant with yellow Fallopian tube-like flowers arising from the stem. Naturally this was used in aiding childbirth.

A constant battle had to be fought against the external and internal parasites of man – fleas, lice, bed-bugs and different types of worm. Many of the plants have flowers or seeds that just look like fleas: louseworts and fleaworts, as well as flukewort and pestilence wort. A lot of these early English names end in "wort", which simply means "a plant", and many of them have a medical prefix: other examples are feverwort, colicwort, goutwort, lungwort and toothwort. It was a long time before belief in these plant associations was finally abandoned.

LE CINQVIEME
FOVRNEAV.

LE TROISIEME
FOVRNEAV.

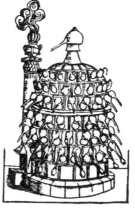

LE DERNIER
FOVRNEAV.

LE SECOND
FOVRNEAV.

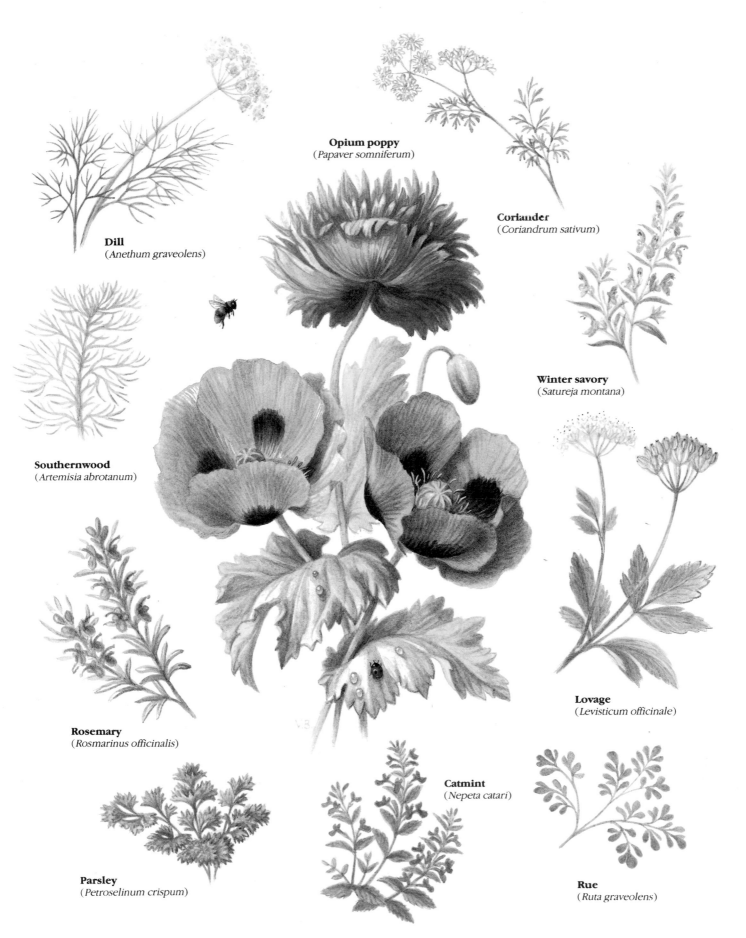

Dill
(*Anethum graveolens*)

Opium poppy
(*Papaver somniferum*)

Coriander
(*Coriandrum sativum*)

Southernwood
(*Artemisia abrotanum*)

Winter savory
(*Satureja montana*)

Rosemary
(*Rosmarinus officinalis*)

Lovage
(*Levisticum officinale*)

Parsley
(*Petroselinum crispum*)

Catmint
(*Nepeta catari*)

Rue
(*Ruta graveolens*)

CHAPTER FOUR

OUTWARD BOUND

(1600 – 1700)

A new generation of gentlemen-botanists evolved in the seventeenth century. Some collected their own plants abroad, others commissioned plant collectors to hunt for interesting new species around the world. Many were supplied by professional nurserymen, anxious to cater for this new demand for the rare and exotic. The arrival of the settlers in North America heralded a busy interchange of plants between the Old World and the New. Growing food crops was the primary consideration for the settlers, but they gradually created sophisticated European-style gardens.

One of the leading naturalists of the period was John Ray, "Father of English Natural History". His researches into all aspects of the natural world set a new, high standard of objective accuracy. As Ray wrote, "Some reproach methinks it is to learned men that there should be so many animals still in the world whose outward shape is not yet taken notice of or described, much less their way of generation, food, manners, uses, observed."

The splendid topiary garden at Levens Hall, Cumbria. It dates back to the late seventeenth century.

After the accession of James I to the English throne in 1603, the influence of Continental ideas became more marked in the development of English gardening. The restrictive rectangular confines of the Elizabethan garden began to give way to much larger, more sweeping designs. As French garden concepts began to develop on separate lines from the classical designs of Renaissance Italy at the beginning of the century, greater emphasis was given to the relationship between the house and garden. The floral knot garden was succeeded by the formal parterre with its elaborate, matching patterns composed almost exclusively of closely clipped box. This formed the centre-piece of the ideal French garden described by Olivier de Serres in 1600 in his *Théâtre d'Agriculture*.

Some of the most elaborate plans might include a whole series of knot or parterre areas, often part of a huge design that would contain mazes and sections for herbs, fruit trees and beds of flowers, low hedges, arbours and screens for climbing plants.

In 1625 Sir Francis Bacon, a keen garden lover who regarded gardening as "the purest of human pleasures . . . the greatest refreshment to the spirits of man", published his essay *Of Gardens*, in which among more formal ideas he advocated a six-acre heath or desert area with "some thickets made only of sweet-briar and honeysuckle, and some wild vine amongst; and the ground set with violets, strawberries, and primroses; for these are sweet, and prosper in the shade".

The importance of vistas began to be emphasized, especially from the house, so that an unimpeded view of the garden with its foreground of a formal parterre and distant views of the countryside beyond its boundaries could be seen from the windows, or from a vantage point in the garden itself. Gravel walks shaded by hedges or tree-lined avenues providing areas for exercise, interspersed by statuary and fountains, became increasingly important features later in the century. The planting of woodland areas came to be appreciated, following the ideas of the celebrated French garden designer, André Le Nôtre, whose influence can be seen in the writings of Sir Thomas Browne and John Evelyn, culminating in Evelyn's publication in 1664 of *Sylva, or a Discourse of Forest Trees*. Two of Charles II's gardeners, John Rose and George London, visited France to see his work. Many garden lovers of the period were influenced by French ideas and after the accession of

Left: *An elaborate design for a summer garden, from De Passe's* Hortus Floridus *(1614).*

Right: *The long view from the château at Vaux-le-Vicomte. Laying out the gardens at Vaux-le-Vicomte in 1650 was one of Le Nôtre's first major works.*

Left: *Collecting cocoons and weaving silk, from a fifteenth-century French manuscript.*

Right: *The garden as a symbol of patience, from George Wither's* Emblemes *(1635).*

to provide) to buy and distribute in your county the number of ten thousand mulberry plants, which shall be deliver'd to you at our City of London, at the rate of three farthings a plant, or at six shillings the hundred".

Although the plants took root, evidence of which is seen in the number of mulberry trees surviving today that can claim direct descent from those originally planted, the scheme proved a failure, for the wrong type of tree had been chosen. Silk worms prefer the white mulberry (*Morus alba*), a native of China, but it was the black mulberry (*Morus nigra*) from Western Asia that had been introduced, and the silk worms did not thrive.

The widespread interest shown in gardening in the first half of the seventeenth century is reflected in the number of publications that appeared. William Lawson's *The Country Housewife's Garden* and *A New Orchard and Garden*, published in 1618, aimed at a humbler market than the owners of the great gardens of grand design, and offered down-to-earth advice on horticultural methods. It was illustrated with woodcuts and included a section on fencing – an important consideration in those days of open common land where hogs and cattle roamed freely. This was followed in 1629 by John Parkinson's *Paradisi in Sole Paradisus Terrestris*, the first book to discuss the aesthetic value of flowers as well as providing useful medicinal tips. Parkinson, an apothecary who became herbalist to James I, was an acute observer and lists about one thousand cultivated plants. He later extended this to 3,800 plants, grouped under their medicinal properties, in his *Theatrum Britannicum*, published in 1640, after he had inherited de L'Obel's records.

A sad loss to scientific advancement was Thomas Johnson (1600-44), who was killed in the Civil War defending Basing Castle. He was a herbalist and a proficient botanist. He revised Gerard's *Herball* in 1633, removing some of its wilder inaccuracies, and in 1634 published *Mercurius botanicus*.

Much has been learned about gardens of the period from Sir Thomas Hanmer's *Garden Book*, written in 1659 but not published until the present century. His plant lists are accurate and detailed. He included 21 different roses and a number of evergreens – known as "greens", and increasingly popular

William and Mary in 1689, Dutch horticultural knowledge and plant imports from the East Indies also became widespread.

At the same time as ideas for garden design were infiltrating from the Continent, plant introductions from all over the world were flooding into the country. Some importations were more successful than others. In the wake of the religious persecutions in France and the Low Countries, James I, anxious to establish a silk industry to provide employment for 40,000 Huguenot refugees, tried to encourage his subjects to plant mulberry trees. He himself experimented with silk production at Hatfield House, Theobalds, and Whitehall Palace. Silk was a valuable commodity in the seventeenth century. Such was its scarcity, Elizabeth I had passed a law forbidding commoners to wear it. In a letter to his Lord Lieutenants of January 19, 1609, James instructed each of them "to pursuade and require such as are of ability, (without descending to trouble the poor, for whom we seek as the century progressed – and his is the first recorded mention of the splendid cedar of Lebanon (*Cedrus libani*).

THE PLANT COLLECTORS

By the middle of the century a new generation of gentlemen-botanists had evolved whose interests lay beyond the spacious vistas and complex parterres of fashionable garden design, and who were seeking a wider choice of plants and experimenting with some of the new, strange specimens that were coming in from abroad. Their needs were met by plant collectors and professional nurserymen, people such as George Ricketts of Hoxton, whom John Rea considered

"the best and most faithful florist now about London", and Captain Leonard Gurle, who supplied Woburn with fruit trees. John Rose, King Charles II's gardener, ran a nursery business as well. These nurserymen published their own lists and catalogues of plants and seeds available.

Probably one of the most renowned of the collectors was John Tradescant the Elder (c. 1570-1638) who was gardener to Robert Cecil, Earl of Salisbury, at Hatfield House, then Lord Wotton of Canterbury, and who finally became Charles I's Keeper of His Majesty's Gardens. He laid out the gardens at Hatfield House for Lord Salisbury. To stock this grand garden Tradescant was asked to visit the Low Countries and purchase plants; some of his bills for 13,000 bulbs and large numbers of fruit trees are still in existence at Hatfield.

Above: *John Tradescant the Elder (c. 1570-1638).*

Left: *The herb garden at the Tradescants' house in Lambeth, London. It was designed in 1982 as a tribute to the Tradescants and planted with a selection of more than thirty herbs that were grown in seventeenth-century English gardens.*

In 1618 with his friend Sir Dudley Digges, Tradescant went on an expedition to Russia, compiling the first-ever list of Russian plants and coming back with numerous specimens, including the white-barked silver birch, a giant form of sorrel, bilberries, strawberries, a geranium and the beautiful larch – that deciduous conifer, destined 300 years later to be an important forestry tree. One of the highlights of the Russian trip was a visit to Rose Island in the Dvina delta, which was smothered with the wild *Rosa cinnamomnea*, "a single rose, wondrous sweet".

Two years later he joined a 24-gun ship as a paid seamen and sailed off to the North African coast to harry pirates who were menacing shipping. In between adventures he was able to acquire plants and seeds, bringing back the Algerian apricot, as well as native and introduced plants of the Mediterranean such as *Gladiolus byzantinus*, narcissus, crosus, colchicum and cistus.

At his home in Lambeth, south of the Thames, Tradescant established his garden. The house was known as the Ark, as his collection of curios from all over the world grew into a museum, later to form the basis of the Ashmolean Museum in Oxford. He was particularly interested in fruit, and in his garden he assembled 57 varieties of plum, 49 kinds each of apple and pear, 24 varieties of cherry, 8 of apricot and 9 nectarine varieties, mostly introduced by himself or his son. In 1634 he published a garden catalogue *Plantarum in Horto*, which listed the names of more than 750 plants. The Ark garden must have been a little enclave of botanical wonder. Many of the garden plants imported to England were first grown there before being distributed to other growers.

Tradescant must have had a continual problem with birds eating his fruit. In *The English Husbandman* of 1613, Gervase Markham recommended employing a young boy with a bow and arrow as a bird-scarer. If he ran up and down "making a great noise and acclamation", this would be the "best and safest means to prevent this evil". The predatory kite (*Milvus milvus*) had been common in London since Tudor times and may also have proved an effective bird-scarer.

John Tradescant junior took over his father's position as "Keeper of His Majesties gardens at Oatlands", and continued to expand the Lambeth botanic collection. He travelled to Virginia on collecting trips in 1637, and in 1642 and 1653 following the death of his father, and introduced many plants that are now familiar in British gardens. Visitors to Virginia were struck by the great heights of the trees growing in forests which stretched right down to the shore. "All the country is overshadowed with trees," wrote William Strachey in about 1612. Tradescant came home with seeds and roots of many of the trees that had impressed him and successfully established them in his Lambeth garden. New introductions included the magnificent tulip tree (*Liriodendron tulipifera*), the red maple, the swamp cypress (*Taxodium distichum*), the American walnut and the sumach.

John Tradescant Junior (1608-62), painted in his garden.

Two trees that had a lasting effect on the course of urban gardening were the false acacia (*Robinia pseudo-acacia*) and, indirectly, the American plane tree (*Platanus occidentalis*). Cuttings of the American plane were raised in the Tradescants' garden, and so were several young Asian plane trees (*Platanus orientalis*). The London plane, *P. x acerifolia*, is a hybrid of these two species and it is commonly believed that the first London plane may have been raised in the Tradescants' garden. Both the false acacia and the London plane are tolerant of pollution and are therefore much favoured in urban parks and gardens. An attractive yellow-leaved variety of the false acacia, *Robinia pseudo-acacia* "Frisia", is now widely grown in gardens, and the London plane is common throughout the Continent as a shade-giving tree.

The Tradescants had imported plants from Virginia for some time prior to the younger John's expeditions. The cardinal flower, *Lobelia cardinalis*, and monardas, as well as the yellow lily (*Lilium canadense*) and Michaelmas daisies, correctly called asters, are familiar border plants today thanks to the Tradescants' introductions. They are credited with being the first to grow Virginia creeper, but their most famous Virginian import was Tradescant's spiderwort, *Tradescantia virginiana*. Parkinson recorded its appearance in his *Paradisi*:

"This Spider-wort is of late knowledge, and for it the Christian world is indebted unto that painfull industrious searcher, and lover of all natures varieties, John Tradescant (who) first received it of a friend, that brought it out of Virginia, thinking it to bee the Silke Grasse that groweth there."

The Tradescants were not the only collectors to establish exotic new plants in the gardens of this period, although they probably operated on the most ambitious scale. Many other keen British gardeners imported plants from other professional collectors, notably from the Dutchman, Guillaume Boel. Boel "in his time a very curious and cunning searcher of simples", as he was described by Parkinson, travelled and sent seeds from Germany and Spain, and lived in Lisbon and Tunis.

Top left: *The tulip tree (Liriodendron tulipifera) with cup-like flowers which turn into delicate fruit baskets surrounded by upright seeds.*

Top right: *The alternative name of naked ladies describes the way these autumn crocuses (Colchicum autumnale) produce flowers without any leaves.*

Bottom left: *The Tradescants gave their name to a familiar group of plants called tradescantias which comprises several species.*

Bottom right: *The bright strident colours of this Lychnis coronaria from southern Europe are typical of lychnises.*

Boel sent various seeds to the amateur grower William Coys at Stubbers in Essex. Coys and Parkinson were rival growers, and when on a trip to Spain at Parkinson's expense Boel sent seeds to Coys Parkinson complained bitterly about Coys having forestalled him with descriptions of these new plants, "while I beate the bush another catcheth and eateth the bird".

One of the plants Coys received from Spain was ivy-leaved toadflax (*Linaria cymbalaria*). This is now a very common plant throughout Europe, naturalized on old walls. Most of the ivy-leaved toadflax in Britain may have descended from the plants at Stubbers. It is a persistent grower and in order to distribute its seeds into cracks in the wall, the plant actually turns towards the wall as it ripens.

It was Coys who first persuaded the yucca to flower in England, in 1604. This was one of the most spectacular plant introductions. The variety Coys grew, the Adam's needle yucca (*Yucca gloriosa*), comes from the desert regions of eastern North America.

Coys also grew potatoes and sweet potatoes at Stubbers and his friend, the botanist John Goodyer (1592-1664), was responsible for distributing the Jerusalem artichoke (*Helianthus tuberosus*) to many gardens, another of the new varieties of vegetables that came in from abroad.

The banana was one of the most exciting fruit introductions in the seventeenth century. Thomas Johnson received a banana plant from Bermuda in 1633, which aroused considerable interest:

"This stalke with the fruit thereon I hanged up in my shop, where it became ripe about the beginning of May, and lasted until June: the pulp or meat was very soft and tender, and it did eate somewhat like a Muske-Melon."

THE SPREAD OF KNOWLEDGE

A man of widespread interests was the renowned naturalist and botanist John Ray (1627-1705), rightly known as 'the father of English natural history'. Son of a blacksmith, his mother was a herbalist and almost certainly kept a small cottage garden full of essential plants, so Ray's interest in nature no doubt started when he was very young. With his mother's encouragement and help from the village parson, he received a grammar school education and was accepted as a student at Cambridge, eventually becoming ordained. He lectured in Greek and mathematics and was Junior Dean of Trinity

Right: Yuccas are American plants. Like Yucca filamentosa, *most yuccas produce a tall spike of white flowers at irregular intervals, often not for many years, but it is not true that they die after flowering. They are pollinated by yucca moths in a symbiotic relationship. Detecting the flowers by their scent, the moths transfer a ball of pollen from one plant to the next in which to lay their eggs.*

College, Cambridge. While there, he became fascinated by the wild flowers of the East Anglian fenland and he grew many of them in his celebrated garden at Trinity, known as the "little" garden. They would probably have included the fenland violet (*Viola stagnina*), now a very rare plant due to the draining of the Fens. His first published work, the *Catalogus Plantarum Angliae*, was based on his researches.

In 1662 Ray resigned his fellowship at Cambridge as a consequence of Restoration changes. One of his students, Francis Willughby, became both his collaborator and sponsor, accompanying him on botanical and natural history trips through Europe. Together they planned a monumental work, a history of the natural world, but Willughby died in 1672 and Ray translated and published Willughby's *Ornithologia* after his death. Ray was a prodigious writer; among his works was *Methodus Plantarum Nova* (1682) and his great *Historia Plantarum Centralis*, containing 3,000 folio paintings of plants of the world, was published in three volumes in 1686, 1688 and 1704.

Hitherto the natural world had been treated with a curious mixture of fact and legend, and little objective attention had been brought to bear on the wonders of natural science. Ray's meticulous observations were to point the way for future scholars. "When men do not know the names and properties of natural objects, and are ready to believe any fanciful superstitions about them, they cannot even see and record accurately."

Above: Three magnificent owls, from Willughby's Ornithologia

Left: These finely detailed paintings of insects are attributed to Claude Aubriet (c. 1665-1742).

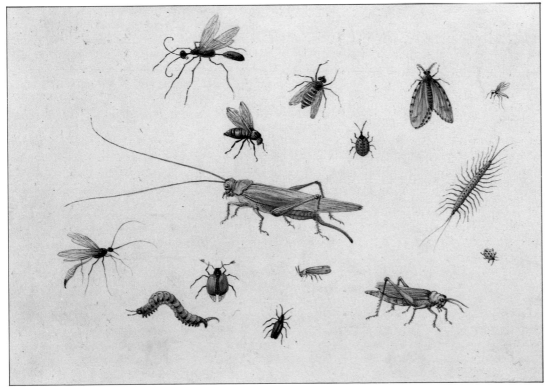

JOHN EVELYN

The Royal Society of London for Improving Natural Knowledge came into existence in about 1645 and received a royal charter in 1662. One of the first Fellows of the Society was the celebrated diarist, John Evelyn (1620-1706). He was a keen horticulturist and created a splendid garden at Sayes Court at Deptford. Evelyn was particularly interested in trees and his book *Sylva, or A Discourse of Forest Trees* (1664), remained the standard work on trees for more than a century.

At Sayes Court Evelyn pursued the investigative ideals encouraged by the Royal Society and besides an "elaboratorye", where he practised chemistry, he included many horticultural features, such as an aviary, a vast orchard with choice fruit trees, a transparent beehive, and a private garden of rare specimen flowers. He also planted over 1,000 specimen trees.

In *Sylva* Evelyn tackled all aspects of the proper propagation, planting and maintenance of trees. He grew some of the new American species, including the tulip tree. This was described in *Sylva* as growing "very well with the Curious amongst us to a considerable Stature. I conceive it was first brought over by John Tradescant, under the Name of the Tuliptree . . . I wish we had more of them; but they are difficult to elevate at first."

John Evelyn (1620-1706).

Evelyn gave detailed instructions for the proper care of oranges: "Never expose your oranges . . . whatever the season flatter, 'til the mulberry puts forth its leafe, then bring them boldly out of the Green-house . . ." These oranges (right) from Pomologie Française (1846), were grown in English gardens by the seventeenth century.

Evelyn was the first writer to describe his orangery as a greenhouse – literally, a structure to shelter tender "greens".

The first building to have been called a greenhouse in Britain was erected at Chatsworth in 1697 by the Duke of Devonshire. It had an arcaded front and a solid roof and was still very similar to an orangery. Evelyn was one of the first gardening writers to note the importance of light for plant growth, declaring that "light is half their (plants') nourishment philosophically considered". Glass had been used in a limited way in orangeries since 1619, but it was some time before the importance of glass roofs was generally accepted.

The hundred-acre garden at Sayes Court contained a number of hedges, notably Evelyn's great holly hedge. He planted the boundaries of the estate with holly in 1670 and one 122 m (400 ft) section was an impressive 2.7 m (9 ft) high and 1.5 m (5 ft) wide. Part of it was damaged in Evelyn's lifetime under rather bizarre circumstances by the Czar of Muscovy. He was a tenant of Sayes Court while Evelyn was away, and persisted in having himself pushed in a wheelbarrow repeatedly through the hedge.

Evelyn was a great advocate of hedges and introduced many interesting hedging plants. He recommended yew as an ideal choice, "preferable, for beauty and a stiff defence, to any plant I have ever seen", and was the first to bring yew hedges into fashion. Among the more exotic species, he suggested tamarisk and yucca. Of yucca, he wrote, "The American Yucca is a hardier plant than we take it to be . . . Why should it not make one of the best and most ornamental fences in the world for our gardens?" On a smaller scale, he recommended chervil as "handsom and proper for the edging of Kitchin Garden beds".

Other Virginian trees grown at Sayes Court included the Virginian cedar, the Virginian walnut and scarlet oak. (*Quercus coccinea*). Among imported American shrubs were yucca, philyrea (his spelling) and American jasmine. In February 1653 Evelyn recorded in his diary: "I planted the orchard at Says Court; new moon, wind west." The mention of the moon is interesting because it reflects the concern with the state of the moon evident in all the gardening "calendars" up to this time. Broadly speaking, sowing and planting were recommended when the moon was waxing; picking and pruning were generally reserved for when the moon was waning.

Like Tradescant, Evelyn experimented with growing scores of varieties of fruit trees and vines, both local and foreign. There were "Lewes red Warden peare, Arundell Peare, Syon Peach, Orleans Peach, Holland Pipin and Morocco Cherry".

One of his publications was *Directions for the Gardiner at Says-Court*, in which precise details and jobs are described throughout the year, even down to an inventory of what should be in the garden shed.

Evelyn's horticultural ideas represented something of a gardening revolution. His interest in studying natural phenomena for its own sake and not in creating a fashionable garden marked a significant change in attitude, and his investigative approach was echoed in the gardens created by other members of the Royal Society. In a letter to his friend Sir Thomas Browne, he wrote of his loathing of gardens "which appeare like Gardens of paste board and March paine and smell more of paynt then of flowers and verdure". He went on to advocate the cultivation of gardens "these innocent, pure, and usefull diversions", as an antidote to the "ruines of our miserable yet dearest country".

Orange de Malte.

368.

Poiteau pinx.!

De l'Imprimerie de Langlois.

Bocourt sculp.!

Tulips and insects, from L'Anglois' Livre des Fleurs *(1620).*

In 1655 John Rea, who died in 1681, published his *Flora, Ceres and Pomona*, a comprehensive and practical gardening book. A big section was given to the tulip which was at the height of its popularity in England. From this work and the *Garden Book* of Rea's contemporary and patron, Sir Thomas Hanmer, a picture can be formed of the average middle-class garden of the time. Rea, too, had little taste for the artificial:

> "As noble fountains, grottoes, statues, etc., are excellent ornaments and marks of magnificence; so all such dead works in gardens, ill done, are little better than blocks in the way to interrupt sight, but not at all to satisfy the understanding. A choice collection of living beauties, rare plants, flowers and fruit, are indeed the wealth, glory and delight of a garden, and the most absolute indications of the owner's ingenuity; whose skill and care is chiefly required in their choice, culture and position."

Among the gardeners of the Restoration period, we are also indebted to Charles Hatton, whose elder brother had inherited the family home of Kirby. From their correspondence we learn much about the state of horticulture at the time. Hatton records the first flowering in England of the tulip tree, in Lord Mordaunt's garden, discusses the grafting of a pear on dwarfing stock – a speciality of English gardeners – and describes Bishop Compton's collection of valuable trees at Fulham, "his oaks from Virginia with chestnut leaves, walnuts from thence bearing flowers . . . *Larix* or larch trees".

THE NEW WORLD

It is perhaps not surprising that so many of the fine trees and striking garden plants that were introduced in the gardens of Europe during the seventeenth century should have originated in Virginia. The tree-rich state was the chosen home of many of the early settlers and the target of European plant collectors such as John Tradescant. Several Virginian plants are now firm favourites in gardens throughout the world. The true Virginia creeper, with its five-fingered leaves (*Parthenocissus quinquefolia*), makes a spectacular colour display against thousands of walls in the autumn, and Virginia stocks (*Malcolmia maritima*), the tall white spikes of Culver's root (*Veronica virginica*) and mertensias are frequently seen in flower beds.

But it was not all a one-way movement. In 1639 settlers in Jamestown who had more than 40 ha (100 acres) of land were required by law to fence their property and plant orchards and gardens. At one point James I had tried to

"Arrival of the English", from Thomas Harriot's A briefe and true report of the new found land of Virginia *(1590). The map shows part of Pamlico Sound, Roanoke Island, the mouth of Albermarle Sound and the Alligator River and part of Currituck Sound, with the Carolina Outer Banks divided into six islands.*

persuade the colonists in Virginia to grow mulberry trees. A new company was specially set up, but it was doomed to failure. One live consignment of silkworms was drowned when the ship was wrecked in 1609, and another died of starvation on another voyage in 1622. In any case, the new Americans were more interested in making money out of growing tobacco than in feeding silkworms.

By the middle of the next century several European tree species such as silver birch, beech, holly, Scots pine, mountain ash and elm as well as the Mediterranean cedar of Lebanon were thriving in Williamsburg, Virginia. And further north, in New England in 1638, English yew, boxwood (*Buxus* spp.), apples, pears and plums were being successfully grown in gardens.

Yew (Taxus baccata), *the oldest growing of any English tree, was planted in churchyards out of respect for the dead. Despite its poisonous green seeds, the American colonists found it useful as an evergreen windbreak that no pests would defoliate.*

The Pilgrim Fathers had landed at Plymouth, New England, in the winter of 1620. They brought with them a precious cargo of seeds, pips, bulbs and nuts, which they planted in March 1621. The early European colonists came to the New World with relatively advanced horticultural ideas and created European-style gardens out of virtually virgin territory.

Growing food was the primary consideration. In the words of the settlers, they had to garden "for meate and medicine". Their gardens were very similar in style to the Elizabethan cottage gardens. Typically, the layouts were rectangular and very symmetrical, with the houses built against the boundary. Apart from vegetables and fruit, the settlers grew as many herbs as they could for medicine and cooking. A few favourite flowers, such as pinks, primroses and periwinkles, were grown in borders largely devoted to herbs.

In the *Chronicles of Massachusetts Bay, 1623-1636*, are listed some of the supplies required to be sent from England: "Wheat, rye, barley, oats, a hogshead of each in the ear; beans, pease, stones of all sorts of fruits, as peaches, plums, filberts, cherries; pear, apple, quince kernels; pomegranates, woad seed, saffron heads, liquorice seed, (roots sent, and madder roots,) potatoes, hop roots, hemp seed, flax seed, against winter, coneys, currant plants, tame turkeys, shoes."

It is interesting to see that potatoes were being brought back to America, and that ancient favourites such as woad, madder and saffron are included; so, too is the exotic pomegranate. The Pilgrims found that the local Indians were good gardeners, with plots of neatly cultivated crops around their huts. The settlers also cultivated many of the plants grown by the Indians, including wild vines and corn.

Some of the herbal remedies used by the Indians were also adopted by the colonists, such as the use of Virginian snakeroot – the local cure for snake bite. The colonists used to carry a small piece of snakeroot with them in case they were bitten. The special aristolochic acids contained in the root worked to reverse the action of the poison, if the wound was sucked out immediately and some crushed snakeroot was rubbed into it. Snakeroot was also taken internally as a tonic and to restore appetite. It had to be administered care-fully, however, as it could cause paralysis, vomiting or diarrhoea if taken in large amounts.

The bark of the Virginian dogwood (American boxwood) was used by the local Creoles to whiten their teeth. The plant came into flower so regularly in the first week of May each year that it was used by the colonists as a reminder to plant their corn seeds. Another local plant that the settlers adopted for medicinal purposes was the parasitic plant called beechdrops (*Epifagus virginiana*), which the Indians used as a cure for all sorts of cancers. They had a cure for syphilis, too. They used blue lobelia, which was later given the name of *Lobelia syphilitica*. The Indians also used the powdered root of white hellebore (*Veratrum viride*) for rubbing into wounds – after they had first rubbed in racoon or wild cat grease.

*Colonists importing new crops such as the redcurrant (*Ribes sativum*) into America were likely to find them defoliated by native insects, like the currant clearwing (*Aegeria tipuliformis*) whose caterpillars bore into the stems. The fruits are devoured by birds.*

For their own remedies, the settlers turned to their herbals. The only herbal known to have been taken over to New England on *The Mayflower* was Dodoens's *Pemptades*, published in Flemish in 1554. Of the several influential herbals published in English in the late sixteenth and early seventeenth centuries, however, it is certain that the colonists used John Gerard's *Herball* (1597), John Parkinson's *Paradisi in Sole, Paradisus terrestris* (1629) and *Theatrum botanicum* (1640), and Nicholas Culpeper's *Physicall Directory* (1649) and *English Physician* (1653).

Culpeper was the herbalist who formulated the Doctrine of Signatures, based on the traditional belief that the appearance of a plant was related to the disease and its cure (see page 62). He was also convinced that there was a mystic link between certain herbs and certain stars. "I prove it thus," he wrote, referring to wormwood, "what delights in Martial places is a Martial herb . . . wormwood delights in Martial places (for about Forges and Ironworks you may gather a cart load of it). Ergo it is a Martial herb." Some of his remedies were a little bizarre, using toads and worms, but as a Puritan himself his views were well received, and his books were widely read by the settlers.

Their rype corne

Their greene corne.

Corne newly sprong.

Their sittinge at meate

The place of solemne prayer.

The howse wherin the Tombe of their Herounds standeth.

SECOTON·

A Ceremony in their prayers wᵗ strange restures and songs dansinge abowt posts carued on the topps lyke mens faces.

"Village of Secoton", from Harriot's briefe and true report . . . of Virginia. Secoton, the chief town of the Secotan Indians, was discovered on 15 July 1585. The drawing shows the neat way in which the Indians cultivated their maize.

Below: White hellebore, from Matthioli's Commentarii (1565).

TAMING THE WILDERNESS

To grow their herbs and crops, the early settlers faced formidable difficulties. Apart from hostile Indians, there were snakes and wild animals such as the wild cat and herds of buffalo to contend with, and their first task was to build strong barriers to protect themselves and their crops and to prevent their own livestock from straying.

Following the advice given in the early gardening books, such as that of Thomas Hill, writing under the name of Didymus Mountain in *The Gardener's Labyrinth* (1571), many of the settlers planted quick-growing hedges. Hill recommended mixed hedges of "wilde Eglantine Bryars", brambles, gooseberries and barberries (berberis). In New England, garden hedges were often a mixture of eglantine and juniper, said to produce an impenetrable barrier in two years. Wild species such as berberis and robinia were also used, and another popular hedging plant was osage orange (*Maclura pomifera*).

Creating gardens and fields out of the wilderness took quite a while to achieve. Forests had to be cleared and the earliest fields were full of stumps and roots. The settlers worked hard, however, and William

Wood's account of life in the New World, *New England's Prospect* (1629), recorded "very good arable ground, and hay grounds, faire Corne-fields, and fruitful Gardens".

Initial cultivation had to be carried out with heavy hoes, since the rough ground could not be worked by ploughs. Edward Johnson's *Wonder Working Providence of Sion's Saviour in New England* (1654), contains an interesting account of the colonists' working methods:

"The Winter's frosts being extracted from the Earth, they fall to tearing up roots and bushes with their howes, even such men as scarce ever set hand to labour before, men of good birth and breeding, but coming through the strength of Christ to war their warfare, readily rush through all difficulties."

Sketches of the settlement on the island of St Croix, in Maine, show houses with neat garden plots. Salad crops and tobacco were grown in raised beds, and in South Carolina a variety of herbs, such as pot marigold, thymé, hyssop and germander were raised

among borders of pinks, periwinkles and primroses.

Not all the early colonists' gardens were simple rectangular plots. Several governors had more elaborately planted estates. John Winthrop Senior (1588-1649), were elected Governor of Massachusetts four times, and his son John (1606-1676), were both keen gardeners. The younger Winthrop was a physician and for medicinal purposes he relied on plants such as elder, wormwood, anise, plantain root and elecampane (*Inula helenium*), which the settlers had introduced. He also imported many seeds, and a bill for July 26, 1631, from Robert Hill of the Three Angels in London, provides an interesting record of typical prices for purchases: "1oz of alisander seed at 2d; ½oz of clary at 3d per oz; ½oz of maudlin seed at 2d". Other orders on the same bill were for "cullumbine (columbine), hollihocks (hollyhocks), orradg (orange) seed, popey (poppy) seeds and spynadg (spinach) seeds".

An eighteenth-century map of the boundary line between Virginia and Carolina.

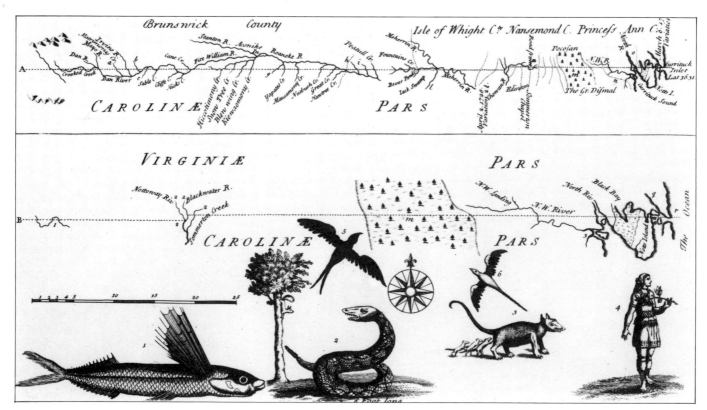

IN THE HEDGEROW

Virgin soil encouraged rampant growth of local plants such as passion flower, mixed with imports such as wild briar and honeysuckle. Plants of the wayside often had important medicinal and culinary uses besides being used to adulterate wine.

Dog rose
(*Rosa canina*)

Ivy-leaved morning glory
(*Ipomoea hederacea*)

Virginian pokeweed
(*Phytolacca americana*)

Passion flower
(*Passiflora incanata*)

Harebell
(*Campanula rotundifolia*)

AGE
OF
ELEGANCE
(1700 – 1800)

This was a period rich in naturalists. Among the most celebrated was the Swedish doctor, Carulus Linnaeus, who devised the system of classification on which all our plant and animal names are now based. On a more modest level, but no less systematic, the Reverend Gilbert White's observations in his *Natural History of Selborne* provide a fascinating picture of gardening methods and the local wildlife in a small corner of rural England.

Early explorers in North America included several distinguished artist-naturalists and their paintings and notes record the many interesting species of flora and fauna they discovered there. Some of the first American presidents were enthusiastic plantsmen. They introduced a host of new species of plants from the countryside and abroad into their own gardens and encouraged other gardeners to be more innovative, too. Plants from North America continued to enrich European gardens. Among the most spectacular introductions were the giant redwoods from California.

*The lake created by "Capability"
Brown at Blenheim Palace,
Oxfordshire.*

The pervading influence of the great French designer, Le Nôtre, the misconceptions of the Renaissance in interpreting classical styles and the stultifying rigidity of Dutch concepts, together with the vogue for trained evergreens, had brought English gardens to a stage where plants had become wholly subordinate to architecture and the dictates of stylized patterns.

> "Our British Gardeners . . . instead of honouring Nature, love to deviate from it as much as possible. Our trees rise in Cones, Globes and Pyramids. We see the Marks of the Scissars upon every Plant and Bush . . . for my own part, I would rather look upon a Tree in all its Luxuriancy and Diffusion of Boughs and Branches than when it is thus cut and Trimmed into a Mathematical Figure."

Joseph Addison was not alone in his opinion. At the time of his article in the *Spectator* of June 25th, 1712, there was a growing revolt, led by the Earl of Shaftesbury, against the extremes of formality that had been reached in garden design at the beginning of the century.

Alexander Pope (1688-1744) lampooned the grosser absurdities in a delightful parody of a gardening catalogue of the period:

> "St George in Box; his arm scarce long enough, but will be in condition to stick the dragon by next April.
> A pair of giants, stunted, to be sold cheap.
> Divers eminent modern poets in bays, somewhat blighted, to be disposed of, a pennyworth.
> A quickset hog, shot up into a porcupine, by its being forgot one week in rainy weather."

When Stephen Switzer, a professional nurseryman from the firm of London and Wise, published his *Ichnographia Rustica* in 1715 he showed the first signs of a less formal approach. This was carried forward by Charles Bridgeman, to whom has been attributed the invention of the ha-ha, considered by many (including Horace Walpole) as the first stage of a gardening revolution by removing the barrier between the garden and the countryside. Irregularity was the keynote; although the straight lines of hedges and gravel walks remained, areas of wilderness – clumps of woodland and cultivated fields – were introduced.

In his design of Rousham, William Kent (1684-1748)

epitomized the spirit of the new movement. Kent had started his career as a sign writer, then became a painter in Rome, and it was through a painter's eyes that his work as a garden designer took shape. Horace Walpole wrote of him, "He leaped the fence, and saw that all nature was a garden." In Kent's hands the straight lines of formal avenues were replaced by serpentine curves; by using the ha-ha he brought the countryside up to the house, combining views and statuary with trees in careful perspective so that each section of the garden offered a fresh vista, each leading to the next in natural progression.

In the 1730s Philip Southcote devised the *ferme ornée* (literally, the "decorated farm"), a combination of garden and practical farm. Both his approach and Kent's signalled the beginnings of an appreciation of nature, romanticized, however, like a painter's landscape. By mid-century the romantic revival was complete and the picturesque style with grottoes, Gothic ruins and classic temples was the height of fashion.

If Kent and Southcote set out to improve on nature by artistic embellishment, Lancelot ("Capability") Brown (1715-83) sought to achieve natural effects through artificial means. His nickname was earned because he was reputed always to see the "capabilities" of an estate for improvement. According to Horace Walpole he had "set up on a few ideas of Kent and Mr Southcote", but the creation of his sweeping landscapes and vast areas of parkland was to have a lasting effect on the British countryside. Exploiting the natural resources of the landscape, planting groves of trees, damming a stream to form a stretch of water in the middle distance, Brown transformed many estates throughout Britain, though this often meant the ruthless destruction of many fine gardens of an earlier period.

His ideas were later modified by Humphry Repton (1752-1818), who restored a refreshing common sense to garden design, bringing a softening influence to the grand landscape concepts of his predecessors. He had little time for the picturesque, seeing in his view of nature not the static scene of a painter but one of infinite variability of light and shade and changing viewpoints. He restored the flower bed to its proper place between the house and the countryside for, he said, "It cannot surely be disputed that some fence should actually exist between a garden and a pasture; for if it is invisible, we must either suppose cattle to be admitted to a garden – or flowers planted in a field; both equally absurd."

A view across the Octagon Pond towards Stowe, Buckinghamshire. Brown was commissioned to landscape Stowe in 1748.

Lancelot 'Capability' Brown (1715-83). Many of his grandest landscape effects were achieved by the destruction of earlier, formalized gardens.

It is a peculiar paradox of the eighteenth century that at a time when exploration and plant collection had expanded rapidly and new plant specimens were arriving on an unprecedented scale, fashion in garden design had turned away from flowers towards landscaped parkland on the grand scale and the flower garden had been banished to a confined area behind high walls well away from the house. It remained for the enthusiastic gardeners and botanists to exploit the new opportunities and for the owners of moderate-sized gardens to experiment with plant introductions and encourage the explorers to venture ever further afield.

MEN OF INFLUENCE

It was a period rich in both amateur and professional naturalists and botanists. One of the most distinguished of all those who contributed to scientific knowledge in the eighteenth century was the celebrated Swedish naturalist, Carulus Linnaeus (Carl von Linné 1707-78). On the binomial system of classification that he devised is founded the principles of all present-day plant and animal nomenclature.

Linnaeus trained in medicine at Uppsala University. Thanks to his father, a Lutheran pastor who was a keen gardener, his first love was botany – by tradition closely associated with medicine – and from an early age he found great satisfaction in the study of plant and animal systems. From this he proved the existence of sexuality in plants and based his classificatory system upon their sexual characteristics – his "lewd and licentious system", as some outraged critics described it.

In 1732 Linnaeus embarked on a remarkable tour of Lapland, covering 4,000 miles under extremely harsh conditions in a wild and dangerous region. Though his account of his travels was not published until the following century, his name was made, and the specimens he brought back were the start of a valuable collection. This was eventually bought from his son Carl after his death by the British naturalist James Edward Smith who brought it to England, where it formed the basis of the Linnaean Society, founded in 1778.

In its heyday in the mid 1740s there was no better stocked garden in Europe than Linnaeus's at Uppsala. It had originally been a university garden established by another important botanist, Olof Rudbeck (1630-1702), whose name is remembered in those marvellous yellow plants of the herbaceous border, the rudbeckias. When Linnaeus took over the garden it was run down – there were a mere 300 species – but he managed to raise the total number of plant species for this small garden to over 3,000.

One of his most treasured exotics was the tea bush (*Camellia sinensis*). He experimented with growing it in the bleak Swedish climate but without success. His attempts to establish a culture of cochineal insects, carefully nurtured all the way from Surinam, also ended in failure when a

Above: *Carulus Linnaeus in Lapp costume, from* Thornton's Temple of Flora *(1799-1807).*

Top right: *A view of Linnaeus' garden at Uppsala, Sweden, from* Horti Upsaliensis *(1745).*

Right: *Carpet bedding of rudbeckias (cone flowers) is bound to attract butterflies hungry for nectar. These plants are native to North America and were originally brought to Europe in the 17th century.*

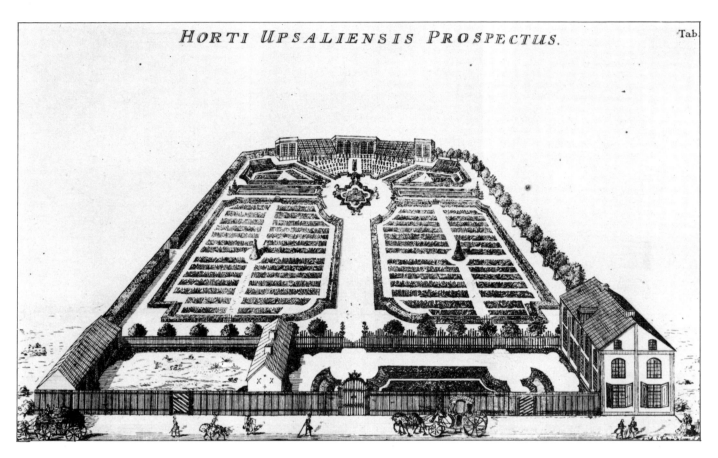

HORTI UPSALIENSIS PROSPECTUS. Tab.

gardener cleaned the insects from the plant they were feeding on. Among the North American species in his garden were Virginia creeper (*Parthenocissus quinquefolia*), ash-leaved maple (*Acer negundo*) and the hop tree or stinking ash (*Ptelea trifoliata*). Linnaeus had hoped to grow bleeding heart (*Dicentra spectabilis*), but what he had in fact was the Siberian corydalis. The bleeding heart is now specially grown in his garden and has naturalized itself in Uppsala.

Among his many publications, the fourth edition of his *Genera Plantarum* which came out in 1752 described nearly 2,000 genera, and in 1753 Linnaeus published his celebrated *Species Plantarum* which covered 7,000 plant species. Linnaeus fitted in his botanizing when he wasn't lecturing at the University. Between 1735 and 1738 he travelled to Holland and then to Germany. In Hamburg he visited the beautiful gardens of Gottfried Jacob Jaenish and Johann Heinrich von Spreckelsen, delighting in their exotic plants and orange trees. He paid a visit to Britain too, meeting Sir Joseph Banks, President of the Royal Society who later became Director of the Royal Botanic Gardens at Kew, and Philip Miller, Director of The Chelsea Physic Garden and author of the *Gardener's Dictionary* (1731-9), one of the standard works of the century. In the seventh edition of 1759 Miller adopted the Linnaean system of nomenclature.

GILBERT WHITE

It may seem strange at first sight that so many naturalists and botanists were either clergymen or doctors. That there is a relationship between medicine and natural history is fairly obvious: scientific curiosity and the necessity of some botanical knowledge in the application of herbs is self-evident. In the case of the parson, his duties were not very onerous and much of his time would be spent in travelling about the parish and tending the spacious garden of a large, rambling house.

Such was the life of Reverend Gilbert White (1720-93), perhaps the most celebrated of all the parson-naturalists, whose *Natural History of Selborne* published in 1789 has never been out of print and has become one of the classic books on natural history of all time. It consists of letters written to White's two naturalist friends, Thomas Pennant and Daines Barrington, on the subject of his observations of wildlife at his home in the Hampshire village of Selborne. Written with publication in mind, the letters are based on a unique 40-year record that White kept of his garden activities at his house, The Wakes, and meticulously detailed natural history notes. These journals consisted of a *Garden Kalendar* from 1751 to 1767, followed by the *Naturalist's Journal*, a more structured daily record of plants, insects, birds and mammals as they came to his notice, and an intensive study of the wild

This sketch of Gilbert White (1720-93) is the only authentic likeness of him.

plants found in the area in the course of one year, 1766, which he called *Flora Selborniensis*.

Written in a clear, lucid style the original journals are rich in information, giving an unprecedented insight into the gardening methods of a modest citizen of the eighteenth century. His enthusiasms capture our imagination across the centuries: the first sighting of the swallows; the behaviour of the field cricket and the successes and failures of his fruit, vegetable and flower gardens; above all his singular pre-occupation with the hot-bed cultivation of melons and cucumbers, a highly popular pastime in the second half of the eighteenth century.

Gilbert White was not only a keen gardener but a true naturalist. He was the first to identify the harvest mouse as a distinct species and made a special study of the noctule bat. Through Daines Barrington his monographs on the hirundines – martins, swallows and swifts – were read before the Royal Society, though as an amateur he received no official recognition and he was far too modest to seek it. *The Natural History of Selborne* remains, however, as his permanent memorial and there is a small museum at his house The Wakes, where the garden has been partially restored and the ha-ha that he built, in keeping with the fashion of the day, can still be seen.

Gilbert White's ha-ha at the Wakes. It was built in 1761 and its construction and cost was recorded in Garden Kalendar. The ha-ha got its name from the surprised cries of "Ah! Ah!" prompted by the sight of sunken ditches, according to one early eighteenth-century garden writer.

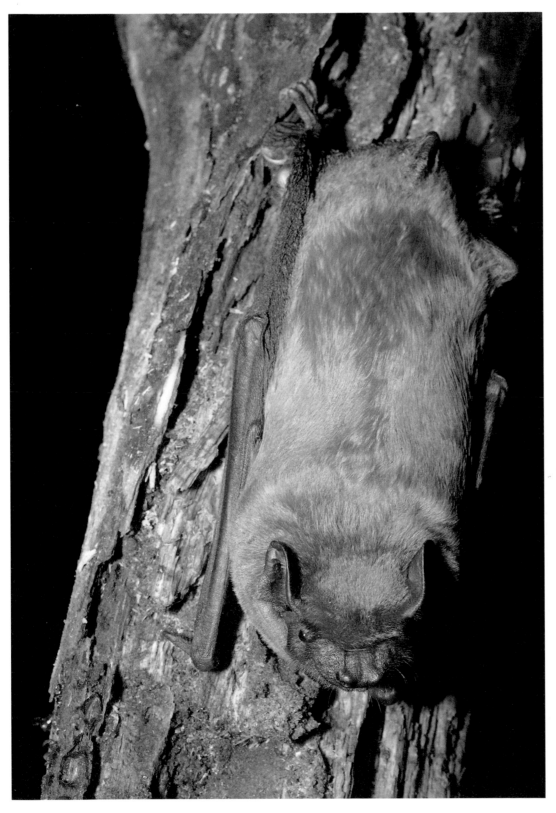

Left: "The great large bat retires and migrates very early in the summer: it also ranges very high for its food, feeding in a different region of the air . . ." So said Gilbert White, describing some of the features of the noctule bat (Nyctalus noctula) This bat only rarely roosts in roofs, more often in tree holes, and is therefore less likely to be caught than several other species.

Below: As their name suggests, harvest mice (Micromys minutus) are traditionally found in cornfields. "They are much smaller and more slender than the mus domesticus medius of Ray; and have more of the squirrel or dormouse colour" observed Gilbert White.

Most notable among the physicians who made a name for themselves as keen naturalist-gardeners was Dr John Fothergill (1712-80), a Quaker. By 1774 he had the largest medical practice in London (in Lombard Street) and had the time, with the help of 15 gardeners, to look after a garden containing 6,500 plant specimens, a quantity second only to that in the Royal Botanic Gardens at Kew. Fothergill's interest in plants was sparked off by another physician, Dr Peter Collinson (1694-1768) whose gardens were at Peckham and later on at the present site of Mill Hill School playing fields.

Fothergill's botanic garden was at Upton House and he stocked it with plants from wherever he could get them. He always visited the London docks to commission seed collection and on one day took the opportunity of befriending a captain suffering from yellow fever, whom everyone else was avoiding, with the object of studying the disease. In lieu of payment Fothergill asked that the man bring back "two barrels of earth from Borneo taken from as many points as possible"; they were duly brought to him, and from these samples Fothergill is said to have germinated several new, but otherwise unnamed, plant species. So successful were his medical skills – he was earning £5,000 per annum in 1774 – that his earnings financed his passion for gardening.

He built a magnificent heated greenhouse, at huge expense, which extended for 80 m (262 ft) and was the envy of everyone, including another successful physician, Sir Joseph Banks (1743-1820), who thought it was the largest he had seen anywhere in Britain or abroad. Fothergill was able to persuade exotic orchids to flower in his new greenhouse. (The first exotic orchid to flower in Britain, incidentally, is said to have been *Bletia verecunda*, from the Bahamas, which a Mr Demidoff achieved in 1731).

Left: *This magnificent East Indian lotus* Nelumbo nucifera *from Asia was sacred in China and India, for it was believed that Buddha was born inside one of these flowers. It is surprising that such a beautiful plant is regarded as a pest in waterways. The other species of* Nelumbo *is the yellow American lotus or water chinquapin (*N. lutea*) from eastern America.*

Right: *Californian dogwood, painted by Marianne North in the nineteenth century. It was first collected by John Tradescant the Elder.*

Right: *Dr John Fothergill (1712-80).*

Left: *The flowers of most gentians are blue, but those of the tall and striking species* Gentiana lutea *are an exception. It grows in great abundance in some alpine meadows and is left untouched by cattle.*

One of the star attractions in the Fothergill greenhouse was The Queen of American Flowers, the water chinquapin *Nelumbo lutea* from the Delaware river. This was a discovery by the American botanist John Bartram, and was sent over in a cask in 1770 for introducing to the canals Fothergill had had made for water plants. As Bartram described it, "She is so coy a lady as not to bear a touch from any other species without fainting." Another botanical gem at Upton was the first-ever tea tree (*Camellia sinensis*) to flower in Britain in 1774. Specimens were eagerly sought by royalty: Queen Charlotte (George III's queen) asked her physician, Dr William Hunter, "to make interest with Dr Fothergill to get her only one of them for Her Majesty's own garden".

Fothergill had collectors in China, Hindustan, the East and West Indies, Siberia, Mexico and North America. In America he financed the two Bartram brothers, John and William, and received many new seeds from Humphrey Marshall, a Pennsylvanian Quaker. With his associate botanist and fellow Quaker, Dr John Lettsom, Fothergill issued detailed instructions to all his plant hunters and sea captains on the best ways of transporting plants, giving specific details of the protective measures to be taken.

> "The captain who takes charge of them must be particularly informed that the chief danger plants are liable to in sea voyages is occasioned by the minute particles of salt water with which the air is charged . . . he therefore should never let the covers be off except on days when the wind is not sufficiently high to beat the water into what the sailors call white caps."

Instructions were also laid down about the best way of preserving seeds to prevent them from rotting or from drying out by enclosing them in beeswax or in waxed paper or linen to keep out the air.

Teaming up with another physician, William Pitcairn (1711-91), Fothergill paid for Thomas Blaikie, one of his former gardeners, to collect plants in the Swiss Alps. Fothergill also maintained a special "wilderness" area, perhaps one of the first to do this professionally with a view to supporting "wild" plants.

Another gardening enthusiast, Sir John Hill (1707-77), was an English apothecary who held a doctorate in botany and was a prolific writer. Gilbert White had recourse to his advice on more than one occasion. His first book *Eden* (1757) advised potential gardeners to make small flower beds in the "natural style". He worked for both Lord Petre and the Duke of Richmond, helping to build up their botanical collections, and in 1759 published *The Vegetable System* jointly with John Stuart, Earl of Bute. Not unusually have people been seen taking cuttings from plants in gardens open to the public, but John Hill was actually banned from visiting the Chelsea Physic Garden in 1744 for taking too many! In 1768 he brought out the first *Hortus Kewensis*, listing all the species planted in the Royal Botanic Garden at Kew.

THE COLLECTION AT KEW

This botanic garden, belonging to Kew House, had been developed by Frederick, Prince of Wales and Princess Augusta, who after his death in 1751 had continued her interest in it with the help and advice of the Earl of Bute, himself an able botanist. William Aiton was appointed gardener, and the fine collection of exotic plants soon became internationally renowned. Even before the retirement of Philip Miller at the Chelsea Physic Garden, Kew had become the chief repository of new species and rare plants, and on his mother's death in 1772 George III brought in the eminent Sir Joseph Banks as Superintendent.

Few keen naturalists could afford to do their own collecting, but Joseph Banks (1743-1820) was the fortunate heir to a £6,000-a-year estate. He went to Newfoundland and Labrador in 1766 and returned with collections of plants and insects. It was he who financed Captain Cook's celebrated voyage of discovery on the *Endeavour* in 1768 at a cost to himself, it has been estimated, of £10,000. Banks was an extremely able man, and was elected Fellow of the Royal Society at the early age of 23. It was at his instigation that it was decided to transport breadfruit trees from Tahiti to the West Indies to provide food for the slaves – a project which resulted in the famous mutiny against Captain Bligh of the *Bounty*. Breadfruit (*Artocarpus incisus*) is now a part of the staple diet in many parts of the Pacific Islands and is grown in gardens.

Banks sailed with Cook to Tahiti, New Zealand and Australia. Following a brief landing at Staten Island off Tierra del Fuego he wrote: "I found about a hundred plants . . . Of these I may say every one was new and entirely different from that either of us had before seen." In Australia he found the Australian honeysuckles (*Banksia* spp.) which were given his name. These now grow in warm Mediterranean gardens, Californian gardens and in the Scilly Isles in Britain.

To the Chelsea Physic Garden, established by The

Above: Sharing its common name with rudbeckias, the black-eyed Susan (Thunbergia alata) is a member of the acanthus family. The black centre to the flowers comprises the reproductive parts.

Right: As director of Kew, Sir Joseph Banks sent plant collectors around the world. The plants they sent back were displayed at Kew. Among the more exotic, was the lotus Nelumbo nucifera.

Worshipful Company of Apothecaries in 1673, Banks gave an enormous amount of basaltic lava from Iceland. This was a creditable attempt to grow plants in an appropriate ecological environment which botanic gardens do today, and ordinary gardeners try to emulate.

Under Banks's direction and careful organization, Kew became recognized as the chief scientific centre for plant cultivation, and in 1789 a second *Hortus Kewensis* was published by Kew's distinguished gardener, William Aiton, which named 5,535 species grown there. For the first time Kew sent out its own collectors. The first professional collector was Francis Masson (1741-1805), who travelled to the Cape of Good Hope in 1772, bringing back species of senecio and the first South African heaths. He also visited Madeira and the Canary Islands, Spain and Portugal and North America. In the course of his travels in Africa, Masson met and became friendly with Carl Peter Thunberg, the Swedish physician and botanist and pupil of Linnaeus who looked after Linnaeus's museum after his death. He is remembered by the genus of plants called *Thunbergia*, which includes the delightful black-eyed Susan.

PLANTS FROM THE NEW WORLD

English physician-gardeners were also practising in the New World. Dr Alexander Garden (ca. 1731-91) was a graduate of Edinburgh University and practised for thirty years in Charleston, Carolina. Here he botanized and collected plants, some of which he sent to plantsmen in England, and among these were gardenias, which were named after him.

Other plants were sent back from the New World to English apothecaries. John Lawson arrived in the Carolinas as a young man from England in 1700 and landed at Charles Town (now Charleston). He became the Surveyor General to North Carolina and went on a 59-day, 966 km (600 mile) journey through beautiful country to an English settlement on the Pamlico river. Here he built a house (and presumably garden) in the area that is now known as New Bern. He was fascinated with flora and fauna and sent seeds, insects and other animals back to London to an apothecary friend, James Petiver (1663/4-1718), himself a noted plant collector. In 1709 he published *New Voyage to Carolina* in which he described the wildlife of the region.

Plants from North America also supplied European kitchen gardens. It is interesting that the familiar strawberry grown in gardens today is the result of a hybridization between the Virginian strawberry (*Fragaria virginiana*) abundant in Virginia, and the *Fragaria chiloensis* long cultivated by the American Indians. They were brought independently to Europe and hybridized accidentally in an Amsterdam garden in 1750.

Not all plants brought to Europe from Virginia and other areas of North America were given an American label. One was the squaw berry, or partridge berry (*Mitchella repens*) which was named after an American doctor who lived in Virginia, Dr John Mitchell (1676-1768). He was a keen botanist who corresponded with Linnaeus. Another doctor in Virginia, Dr Charles Amson, is remembered by a group of shrubs called *Amsonia*, species of which are found both in North America and Japan.

As the settlers and adventurers moved further inland from the eastern coasts of America, they made inroads into the extensive natural deciduous forest. There was a huge forest, 1,288 km (800 miles) wide, from the St Lawrence in the north to Louisiana in the south, full of new and interesting species. In great pioneering and botanical style, as each of the new American states were formed they adopted a native tree species for their logos. This gives us a good idea where some of the species that were to transform the forestry of the countryside and colour our gardens originally came from.

DEVELOPMENT OF AMERICAN GARDENS

It was not until the end of the seventeenth century that the western coast of North America began to be opened up, when the Jesuits settled in Baja, California, and began to cultivate the inhospitable land. Before that, practically no one had explored the colourful Californian coast. Various explorers had visited the harbour which is now surrounded by San

---

PLANTS FROM VIRGINIA

Choke cherry (*Prunus virginiana*)

Common spiderwort
  (*Tradescantia virginiana*)

Culver's root, blackroot
  (*Veronica virginica*)

Hop hornbeam (*Ostrya virginiana*)

Juniper, Pencil, Red Cedar, or
  Virginia Cedar
  (*Juniperus virginiana*)

Persimmon (*Diospyros virginiana*)

Tulip, or Virgin tree
  (*Liriodendron tulipifera*)

Virginian cowslip, or bluebell
  (*Mertensia virginica*)

Virginia creeper
  (*Parthenocissus quinquefolia*)

Tulip, or Virgin tree

Virginian dogwood
  (*Cornus florida*)

Virginian pokeweed
  (*Phytolacca americana*)

Virginian prune (*Prunus serotina*)

Virginian bird cherry
  (*Prunus virginiana*)

Virginian snakeroot
  (*Aristolochia serpentaria*)

Virginian strawberry
  (*Fragaria virginiana*)

Virginian walnut, often confused
  as the hickory
  (*Carya* spp.; two species)

Virginian water horehound
  (*Lycopus virginicus*)

Cloches, bell-jars and wall screens feature in this splendidly formal eighteenth-century kitchen garden. Strawberries and marrows were among the fruits and vegetables from America that were grown in European kitchen gardens at this time.

NORTH AMERICAN EXPLORERS

One of the early naturalists and explorers in the New World was Mark Catesby (1706?-67). He explored Carolina during 1722-5, when the inhabited parts extended only 96 km (60 miles) inland and along the entire length of the coast. He encountered "buffello's", bears, panthers and other wild beasts, but he was primarily interested in trees and shrubs which could be used for joinery, agriculture, food and medicine.

Catesby painted much of what he saw from nature, pretending that he "was not a bred painter", but his collection of watercolours (dated c. 1724), which are now in the Royal Library at Windsor (nobody knows how they got there), give us a fascinating insight into North American wildlife. The colonists lived at the edge of the forest, so much of the wildlife would have ventured into their gardens. Catesby also published *Hortus Americanus or a Collection of 85 curious trees and shrubs, the produce of North America* in 1767.

In August 1743 the Quaker naturalist John Bartram travelled north along the stony and precipitous Appalachian mountains from Pennsylvania to New York. He dined on venison with Indians and saw plenty of interesting plants: linden poplar, elms, oaks, his first American ginseng (*Panax quinquefolius*),

honeysuckles (*Lonicera* spp.), spruce, pine, chestnut (*Aesculus* spp.) and abundant huckleberries (*Gaylussacia* spp.) which on several occasions he stopped to eat. A rattlesnake had to be killed and a singing great green grasshopper was noted in Bartram's *Observations* (1751) as the first he had heard that year. A few years later, in 1774-5 whilst he was travelling alone in Cherokee country, he witnessed a massed aggregation of crocodiles on the St John's river where the water was concentrated through a narrow pass. Here the crocodiles were feasting on the bountiful supply of fish running down river. At one point he came across a natural garden of wild flowers and animals.

Bartram also drew a lot of what he saw and his composite pictures – almost naturalist's sketches with annotations – such as the cardinal or "red bird or Virginian nightingale", myrtle warbler, eastern coach whip snake and ruby-throated hummingbird all vividly reflect wildlife in Carolina. He depicts a typical alligator hole – a place where alligators live during the summer – which is probably the famous Blue Sink in Florida. It is likely that many of these paintings were drawn while he was staying at his uncle's plantation in North Carolina. In 1769 he was residing in Pennsylvania where he had a famous garden.

The two Bartram brothers, John and William, both Quakers, made a big impact on American gardening. Their grandfather had originally emigrated from England in 1682 and both made expeditions in Indian country in search of flowers. The two brothers built up probably the finest collection of native plants in America. Benjamin Franklin, the American philosopher and statesman, was a close colleague. William Bartram (1739-1823) corresponded with many notable botanists in Europe, including Dr John Fothergill and Carl Linnaeus, who is quoted as saying that John Bartram was "the greatest naturalist on Earth".

At about this time a celebrated Dutch naturalist, Baron Nicolas-Joseph Jacquin (1727-181/), made some discoveries in his travels in the West Indies and South America of plants which would become adapted for gardens. He was formerly a professor of botany and chemistry at the University of Vienna before exploring and painting much of what he saw. Some of his paintings are now in the British Museum. Amongst these are the passion flower – a plant the Puritans took very seriously. To them its three styles, five stamens and ten parts of the perianth symbolized the nails of the crucifixion, five wounds and the ten Apostles with the exception of Peter and Judas. Hence the plant's name.

Left: Baron Nicolas-Joseph Jacquin's magnificent painting of a passion flower (1780).

Right: Painted finch, by Mark Catesby (c. 1724).

Diego; Cabrillo in 1542 and Sir Francis Drake 37 years later. Throughout the sixteenth century the Spanish had plied the coasts looking for the fabled Garden of Eden but few had ventured inland, though the mariners were much impressed by what they saw. At what is now called Altadena the countryside blazed with millions of poppies; ships apparently set their course from this natural floral display which could be seen 56 km (35 miles) away!

Once the Jesuits had established irrigation the bare ground blossomed in this warm, Mediterranean-like climate with its huge variety of trees, shrubs and wild flowers. The whole area was under the influence of Spain and Mexico and thirty-two stations and sixteen missions were established. Cultivation of crops and flowers for the altars of these Jesuits flourished for a hundred years. Their gardens were a naturalist's delight, even if sometimes they were ravaged by ground squirrels and gopher tortoises. Missions grew citrons, cotton, dates, figs, grapes, melons, oranges, pomegranates and squashes. They had fine orchards and vineyards and their gardens blossomed with scores of colourful species –

carnations, cornflowers, buttercups, daffodils, gillyflowers, honeysuckle, hyacinths, jasmine, jonquils, lilies, marguerites, sweet williams and roses. The trees and shrubs included carob, blackthorn, cypress, dogwood, laurel, pistachio, juniper and oak.

On their expeditions into the countryside the Jesuits saw the wild roses which reminded them so much of their beloved Rose of Castile. In fact the rose growing wild in the Californian countryside was almost certainly *Rosa californica*. The Castile rose was the Damask rose *Rosa damascena trigintapetala* which was actually the first rose brought into California, not by the Spanish, but by Captain J. F. G. de La Pérouse in 1785.

We owe much of our knowledge about these early Californian mission gardens to the Franciscan friar, Juan Crespi, a lover of nature, who kept an interesting botanical diary. A few of the mission gardens are open to the public today and it is claimed that the mission grapes, figs and olives are directly descended from the original ones planted by the Franciscans, who had taken control from the Jesuits.

Above: *A nineteenth-century painting of a monkey puzzle tree with wild llamas in Chile, by Marianne North.*

Left: *The Carmel Mission, California. Much of California is sub-tropical and the soil is very fertile, so almost everything thrives.*

Towards the end of the seventeenth century there were only three ports open on the Californian coast for visiting ships: Monterey, Santa Barbara and San Diego. Through these, imported plants crossed with exported ones bound for the Old World and beyond.

In 1785 the La Pérouse expedition sailed from France with the botanist Collignon on board ready to collect Californian plants. He found the rose-coloured sand verbena (*Abronia umbellata*) which is reputed to be the first plant ever introduced to the Old World from California. Another botanist on this expedition was Thaddeus Haenke who introduced the California fuchsia to European herbaceous borders. Not a true fuchsia, its Latin name *Zauschneria californica* honours the Bohemian professor of natural history, Johann Baptiste Zauschner (1737-99). Galleons from the Philippines were also crossing to California and trading goods and brought plants such as Banksia roses and loquats from across the Pacific.

In 1791 Captain George Vancouver set sail from England on a voyage of discovery, visiting Australia and New Zealand and in 1792 reaching the Californian coast. He was accompanied by the Scottish botanist, Archibald Menzies (1754-1842) who collected the Californian redwoods (*Sequoia sempervirens*) and the tall Wellingtonia (*Sequoiadendron giganteum*), which were known as the oldest and tallest trees in the world and were much planted in the estates of large houses. (The oldest tree now known is American, the bristlecone pine *Pinus aristata* from Utah, at 4,500 years.) Eventually becoming the tallest vegetation in an area, redwoods are frequently decapitated from lightning attacks. Incidentally they have fireproof bark!

One of the plants brought back to Europe by Archibald Menzies from the west coast of America was the monkey puzzle tree (*Araucaria araucana*). The monkey puzzle is so named because it is thought that monkeys are unable to climb the tree because of its spiky, tough leaves. The apocryphal story is told that Menzies was dining on board ship when the Captain passed round a tray of nuts. Not recognizing which species they were, he slipped a few into his pocket and eventually brought them back to England, germinating them on the way. Sir Joseph Banks was given some of those first trees.

Many a fine garden or churchyard in Europe contains the tall Monterey cypress (*Cupressus macrocarpa*), a legacy from the New World. Hardly any row of gardens in Europe is without the quick-growing *Cupressocyparis leylandii*, which is neither true cupressus nor a false cypress, but a hybrid of the two. It originated in Welshpool in 1888 and is now cultivated by the million to satisfy demand. The Monterey pine (*Pinus radiata*) and the bishop pine (*Pinus muricata*) from California are both found occasionally in formal gardens. The bishop pine gets its name from the Californian place of San Luis Obispo, where it was found much later in 1832 by the collector, Coulter.

In the eastern states of North America, the wealthy Europeans who had settled in Massachusetts created houses and gardens in the English manor house style, complete with knot gardens. In Pennsylvania, William Penn, (1644-1718), the Quaker founder of the state, built a spectacular garden at Pennsbury at enormous cost and had gardeners and seed brought over from England. His lawn was sown specially with English grasses and he introduced wild plants from the local forests.

Thanks to the Dutch and their trading ships, all sorts of plants from different continents began to enrich American gardens. The banks of the Hudson river and Long Island soon came ablaze with the spring blossoms of peaches, pears and cherries and China asters (*Callistephus chinensis*), French and African marigolds (*Tagetes* spp.), celosia and globe amaranth (*Gomphrena globosa*). Crown imperial (*Fritillaria imperialis*) and snake's head fritillaries (*Fritillaria meleagris*) and Martagon lilies (*Lilium martagon*) were mixed with indigenous plants collected from the countryside, such as the orange wood lily (*Lilium philadelphicum*), the Canada lily (*Lilium canadense*) and the flowering dogwood (*Cornus florida*). Other North American species included asters, coreopsis, gaillardias, blue and summer phlox, and southern evergreen magnolia.

Virginian gardens soon blossomed in a golden age of plant introductions. It was a Royalist colony and kept in close contact with England, nurturing the English custom of gardening. The new capital, Williamsburg, became a centre of eighteenth-century life. Large estates were laid out each with large gardens, some of which survive or have been re-created today – Shirley, the home of the presidential family of Carters since 1723; Berkeley, the home of the Harrisons which produced two Presidents, William Henry Harrison (1773-1841) and his grandson Benjamin Harrison (1833-1901); and Westover of the Byrd family. William Byrd (1674-1744) was one of the first men of letters in this part of America and lived a rich colonial life, Westover becoming the "quintescence of Virginia aristocracy". He was a brave explorer, too, walking the 260 km (162 mile) dividing line between Virginia and North Carolina with a group of surveyors.

In his *Westover Manuscripts* (published in 1841) William Byrd recalls how he traversed the Great Dismal Swamp. "It was full of juniper trees, commonly so call'd, tho' they seem rather to be white cedars . . . the ground was generally very quaggy . . . a large tract of reeds . . ." Hogs and cattle were round the edge but no animals were seen in the centre. This was the sort of terrain in which collectors were to find new tree and shrub species which would be brought back to European gardens.

Virginian settlers were becoming rich with their tobacco

An eighteenth-century-style garden at Williamsburg, Virginia.

profits and some fine houses were being built. In the warmer climate of Georgia and South Carolina rice was becoming a staple crop. One of the oldest colonial houses in America still remaining today is Middleton Place, near Charleston. Its landscaped gardens were laid out in 1741. But even this is not the oldest known house and garden in America. In 1985 the evidence of a much older garden was found by aerial reconnaissance at Bacons Castle, 19 km (12 miles) south of Williamsburg. The garden dates from 1680 and is in the English Renaissance style. It has been compared to the garden of Wilton House near Salisbury in England, built for the Earl of Pembroke. From the air it is possible to see several long arbours and numerous flower beds.

Left: *Crown imperial fritillaries (Fritillaria imperialis) were known in gardens before 1590. They were favourites of Dutch flower painters and figured in several books of the 17th century.*

Below: *An elegant parterre at Charleston, South Carolina.*

Henry Middleton (1717-84), speaker of the Assembly in 1745-47 and again in 1754-55, started to build Middleton Place in South Carolina and lay out the grounds in 1740. Using 100 negro slaves, it took about nine years to complete. There were familiar English embellishments: a bowling green, a typical Tudor "mount", flower beds in the form of a spoked wheel, a pair of "butterfly lakes" and avenues of oak and cypresses. One massive "Middleton Oak" remains today and the older trees are festooned with Spanish moss typical of these southern states.

One naturalist who visited Middleton was the Frenchman, André Michaux (1746-1802), who presented the owner with camellias. Michaux had previously botanized in England, the Auvergne in France and in the Pyrenees and North Spain during 1779-80. He had also collected plants in Persia for two years before coming to North America in search of plants in 1785. He was responsible for introducing into America several popular plants which soon became part of colonial gardens: *Azalea indica, Camellia japonica,* crape myrtle (*Lagerstroemia indica*), pink silk tree (*Albizia julibrissin*) and the China-berry (*Melia azedarach*).

The plans of new towns of this time show grand houses, each with their garden plots. Some of the useful plants of the countryside would have been grown here. A 1734 print of Savannah, on the South Carolina/Georgia boundary, shows a well laid-out town plan with neat houses, each with a small parcel of garden. The whole town is hemmed in with virgin forest on three sides and a 12 m (39 ft) bluff on the other side down to the river, also called the Savannah. The birds of the forest would have undoubtedly visited some gardens and many a medicinal plant would have been planted there.

New York gardens had come a long way since the beginning of the seventeenth century when the fortified New Amsterdam was established on the end of Manhattan Island. A contemporary map shows that within the fortified walls (the northern boundary is present-day Wall Street) there were numerous large and formal gardens planted with orchards or arbours.

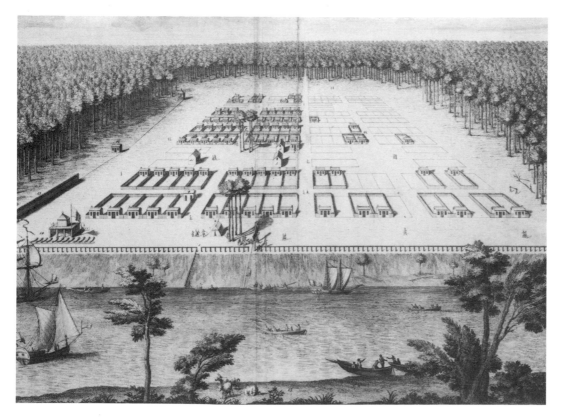

Above: *The attractive Persian acacia or silk tree, Albizia julibrissin, is named after Filippo degli Albizzi who introduced it to Europe in the mid-18th century. In Africa its seeds only germinate after being scorched by fire.*

Left: *A view of Savannah, by Peter Gordon (1734). The town grew very rapidly; in 1745 it had "very near 350 houses . . ."*

CALIFORNIAN GARDEN PLANTS

Bishop pine (*Pinus muricata*)

Californian olive
  (*Umbellularia californica*)

Californian black oak
  (*Quercus kelloggii*)

Californian buckeye
  (*Aesculus californica*)

Californian live oak
  (*Quercus agrifolia*)

Californian fuchsia
  (*Zauschneria californica*)

Californian glory
  (*Fremontodendron californicum*)

Californian lilac
  (*Ceanothus arboreus*)

Californian mock orange
  (*Carpenteria californica*)

Californian poppy.

Californian nutmeg
  (*Torreya californica*)

Californian palm
  (*Washingtonia filifera*)

Californian poppy
  (*Eschscholzia californica*)

Californian redwood
  (*Sequoia sempervirens*)

Californian rose (*Rosa californica*)

Californian walnut
  (*Juglans californica*)

Monterey cypress
  (*Cupressus macrocarpa*)

Monterey pine (*Pinus radiata*)

NORTH AMERICAN FLOWERS

Cardinal flower.

American arrowhead
  (*Sagittaria rigida*)

American crab (*Malus coronaria*)

American cranberry
  (*Vaccinium macrocarpum*)

American elm (*Ulmus americana*)

American raspberry
  (*Rubus occidentalis*)

American viburnum
  (*Viburnum trilobum*)

Canadian pondweed
  (*Elodea canadensis*)

Eastern hemlock (*Tsuga canadensis*)

Golden rod (*Solidago canadensis*)

Honey locust (*Gleditsia triacanthos*)

Lobelia (*Lobelia cardinalis*)

New England aster
  (*Aster novae-angliae*)

New Jersey Tea
  (*Ceanothus americanus*)

Red acer (*Acer rubrum*)

Scarlet oak (*Quercus coccinea*)

Sidalcea (*Sidalcea malviflora*)

Stag's horn sumach (*Rhus typhina*)

Sweet gum (*Liquidambar styraciflua*)

Sidalcea.

PRESIDENTIAL GARDENS

Three successive presidents of America were keen gardeners. George Washington (1732-99) created a marvellous retreat at Mt. Vernon on the banks of the Potomac river, though he rarely used it. It was typically English, with lawns, shrubberies and flower beds. He had a particular interest in trees and shrubs and planted species such as cedar, crab apple, dogwood (*Cornus* spp.), holly (*Ilex* spp.), poplar (*Populus* spp.), laurel (*Laurus* spp.), sassafras (*Sassafras albidum*) and weeping willow (*Salix babylonica*). An orangery and small botanic garden were also made, since Washington had friends who shared his interest in plants, one of whom was John Bartram of Philadelphia who sent him a consignment of some 196 items. One of the earliest botanic gardens in Virginia had been made by John Clayton in the early part of the eighteenth century, but this was later destroyed by the British.

George Washington (1732-99), President of the United States from 1789-97.
Below: *Mount Vernon, Washington. The garden still features the boxwood parterres laid out in the late eighteenth century.*

The third president of America, Thomas Jefferson (1743-1826), was known as the architect-gardener, since he laid out Jefferson City and designed the University of Virginia. He had stayed in Paris as a minister from 1744-89 and was influenced by French architecture. Jefferson was not impressed with English architecture on his 1786 visit but he did praise English parks such as those at Blenheim, Chiswick and Stowe, and he also visited German gardens. Back in America he lavished expense on his Monticello estate and gardens.

On the family estate in 1768 Jefferson set about landscaping a forested mountainside to create his dream home with grounds modelled in the English style. When he became President in 1801 the Palladian-style house was virtually finished but much still had to be done in the garden. Wherever he travelled he sent back waggon-loads of plants.

Jefferson's garden was a flowery one, with tulips, hyacinths, narcissi and bloodroot (*Sanguinaria canadensis*), otherwise called Red Indian paint, since the Indian warriors used the plant for their war paints; it was also used as a tonic and sedative. He also grew poppies, lychnis, cardinal flowers (*Lobelia cardinalis*), St James's lilies and Mexican bulbs. Shrubberies and shady walks were a feature rather than parterres or box hedges. From one of his letters we know that he intended to plant red cedar, evergreen privet, pyracantha and Scotch broom. Keen to learn all about Von Humboldt's latest discoveries in the Amazon, Jefferson invited him to stay for three weeks.

Like a good naturalist-botanist, Jefferson kept a gardening notebook from 1766-1824, in which he listed all the species in his garden. There were at least 89 trees, 64 shrubs, 154 annuals, perennials, bulbs and roots and 16 roses. Today the garden is open to the public.

"No occupation is so delightful to me as the culture of the earth, and no culture comparable to that of the garden. I am still devoted to the garden. But though an old man, I am but a young gardener."

The fourth president, James Madison (1751-1836), also spent a fortune on his Montpellier house in Virginia. The rose gardens, topiary and terraced perennial and annual beds were designed by Pierre L'Enfant, who also planned the City of Washington. When he retired to his Montpellier home Madison was almost ruined, since he had spent so much on the garden and entertainments there.

Thomas Jefferson (1743-1826), President of the United States from 1801-09.

Left: *Monticello, Virginia. "Monticello" is Italian for "little mountain" and the gardens slope down from the level lawn that surrounds the house at the top of the hill.*

The vogue for having extravagant presidential gardens spread to the fifth president, James Monroe (1758-1831) who retired to Oak Hill in Loudoun County in Virginia where, like the others, he indulged in gentlemanly gardening and farming. The seventh, and very boisterous president, Andrew Jackson (1767-1845), lived at The Hermitage, near Nashville, Tennessee, a fine house with grounds specially designed by an Englishman, William Frost in 1819. It was in typical English style (despite the fact that Jackson had a life-long hatred of Great Britain, since he had once received a British sabre wound) and was planted with spring bulbs, peonies, irises, lilies, roses, snowballs (*Viburnum* spp.) and crape myrtles.

Peonies are named after the Greek physician Paeon. Herbaceous peonies are known to have been cultivated in China from the 5th century B.C. This is Paeonia lactiflora.

CHAPTER SIX

THE
CENTURY
OF FLOWERS
(1800 – 1900)

As horizons broadened, plant collectors travelled even further afield in search of the new and exotic. Tea plants were introduced into India from China, thus founding the Indian tea industry; rhododendrons were brought to Europe from the Himalayas and were soon established as the most fashionable plants to grow. The development of the Wardian case ensured a much higher survival rate of plants in transit and sparked off a new boom in plant collection. More naturalistic gardens were created to display the greater choice of plants available most effectively.

Some of our leading naturalists were working in the nineteenth century. In England, Charles Darwin formulated his revolutionary theories on evolution, influenced by his own close observations of flora and fauna patterns in his own garden. In France, the naturalist Jean Henri Fabre's detailed researches on insects observed in and around his garden, still provide the basis of much current thinking.

The Italian Garden at Shrubland Park, Suffolk, from E. Brooke's The Gardens of England *(1857).*

If the eighteenth century saw the eclipse of detail in the interests of picturesque landscapes and noble vistas, the next hundred years might be described as the century of flowers. After the death of Humphry Repton in 1816 no distinctive gardening style emerged for some time, but already there was a move away from the unadorned landscape, as the influence of plant collectors and the proliferation of new botanical species gradually changed the face of British gardens, and brought the emphasis to bear on the plants themselves. Already in 1816 Maria Jackson was advocating in her *Florist's Manual* the addition of beds of flowers to a landscape setting.

NEW INVENTIONS

By the 1830s other factors were contributing to a change in gardening styles. Most notable was the development and marked improvement in the construction of greenhouses, no longer simple lean-tos against the garden wall. An outstanding example was the huge greenhouse designed by Joseph Paxton (1801-65) at Chatsworth, based upon the structure of a water-lily leaf, and which he was to develop further into the triumphant edifice of glass and ironwork which housed the Great Exhibition in 1851.

With much improved glazing and the development of heating facilities provided by steam or hot-water pipes instead of an open stove, it had become possible to cultivate many more of the exotic plants newly introduced every year, and to raise half-hardy bedding plants such as geraniums (pelargoniums) on an unprecedented scale. Carpet bedding, with massed groups of flowers in blazing colours, became commonplace and a degree of formality returned to British gardens with the revival of regularized parterres and beds in geometric patterns cut out of the grass and filled with bedding plants, often in haphazard order with little sense of overall design. As was remarked in the Encyclopedia Britannica of 1838, ". . . respecting the situation of a flower garden, no very precise directions can be given".

In the wake of the industrial revolution and the growth of a prosperous, well-educated middle class, interest was widespread in the smaller, simpler kind of garden, ranging from the neat plot round an urban villa to the modest estate of the new industrialists. To cater for this awakening interest came the first of the gardening magazines and books aimed especially at this new readership. Foremost among these were the works of J.C. Loudon and his wife Jane; his *Encyclopedia of Gardening* came out in 1822 and in 1826 Loudon published the first issue of *The Gardener's Magazine*, which continued until his death in 1843. *The Suburban Gardener and Villa Companion* followed in 1838, and Mrs Loudon brought out *The Ladies' Companion to the Flower Garden* in 1841.

In the *Suburban Gardener* Loudon describes clearly the current emphasis on displaying plants for their own sake, calling it the "gardenesque" style:

"By the gardenesque style is to be understood the production of that kind of scenery which is best calculated to display the individual beauty of trees, shrubs and plants in a state of nature; the smoothness and greenness of lawns; and the smooth surfaces, curved directions, dryness and firmness of gravel walks; in short, it is calculated for displaying the art of the gardener."

The formation of the Horticultural Society in 1804 provided a focus for botanists and horticulturists. The Society aimed to make careful selections of the best forms of plants, and an experimental garden was started first at Kensington and then at Chiswick. It received its charter in 1809, and became the Royal Horticultural Society in 1861.

With the accession of George IV, who had little interest in horticulture, the garden at Kew had become neglected and in 1840 a Committee was set up by Parliament which transferred its administration from the Crown to the Commissioners of Woods and Forests. Sir William Jackson Hooker was appointed its first official Director.

One other factor that brought about a significant development in the cultivation of plants in the nineteenth century was the invention by Dr Nathaniel Bagshaw Ward (1791-1868) of the Wardian case, a glazed compartment for controlling plant growth. Dr Ward discovered this novel technique accidentally while keeping an insect chrysalis safe under a glass dome. Thinking that the insect would soon emerge, he noticed that seedlings were beginning to germinate in the soil in which the chrysalis was kept, and that they were of plants which would not normally survive in the dry air of a room. He conducted further experiments on growing plants under air-tight conditions and in 1842 published the fruits of his research in a booklet called *On the Growth of Plants in Closely Glazed Cases*. The method was now set for transporting plants all round the world instead of leaving them

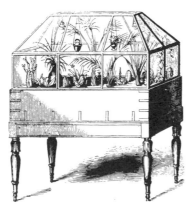

Above: *Compiège in northern France. "Carpet bedding . . . is comparatively a modern idea, and one which has many points that render its adoption to a moderate extent desirable . . ." wrote Robert Thompson in 1881.*

Right: *A Wardian case, from* Every Lady her Own Flower Gardener *(1845).*

to the perils of being tied down on ships' decks and subjected to all the elements. Plants were successfully taken in Wardian Cases to Australia in 1833.

One of the first collectors to use the Wardian case in practice was Robert Fortune (1812-88), who went out to China on behalf of the Horticultural Society in 1843 with explicit instructions to "bear in mind that hardy plants are of the first importance to the Society, and that the value of the plants diminishes as the heat required to cultivate them increases". With the aid of the Wardian case he succeeded in transporting tea plants from China to India and thus founded the Indian tea industry. Through Ward's invention, quinine-producing plants (*Cinchona* spp.) to fight malaria were imported into Europe from the New World and the banana (*Musa* spp.) was introduced from China to the rest of Asia and Africa.

COLLECTORS' ACHIEVEMENTS

The work of two collectors in particular had a profound impact on the appearance of British gardens of the nineteenth century. In 1825 the Horticultural Society sent David Douglas (1799-1834) to California to collect specimens of the plants Archibald Menzies had discovered on his voyage with Vancouver in 1791. Douglas, a young man of great courage, made three journeys between 1825 and 1834 and travelled thousands of kilometres in trackless country. He was responsible for scores of plants that we take for granted in our gardens today – various species of lupins, maples, penstemons and clarkias, Oregon grape (*Mahonia aquifolium*) and flowering currant (*Ribes sanguineum*) and, of course, the Douglas fir (*Pseudotsuga menziesii*) and sitka spruce (*Picea sitchensis*), both tall species more at home in parks, gardens and arboreta. Perhaps gardeners today would remember him more by two other plants that he introduced to gardens, the winter-flowering *Garrya elliptica* and the poached egg plant (*Limnanthes douglasii*) which is a popular and invasive plant of the herbaceous border. On his last expedition in 1834 Douglas met a tragic end while plant hunting on the island of Hawaii. He fell into a camouflaged cattle pit and was found gored to death by a wild bull. Though rumours spread that he had been murdered, there is no evidence to suggest this, and it must be assumed that he had fallen in accidentally. He was only 35.

During the nineteenth century many more naturalists and botanists were pushing their way through the virgin territory of North America and discovering new plants.

George Don the younger (1798-1856) was sent out by the Horticultural Society in 1822. He came from Scotland and had gardening experience at the Chelsea Physic Garden. In 1822 he set sail on rather a fast expedition of the period, calling in at Madeira, Tenerife, Cape Verde Islands, Gambia, St Thomas Island, Sierra Leone, Brazil, Trinidad, Cuba and finally New York, spending 14 months and collecting all the way. Wherever he stopped he would visit the local gardens and, off the coast of Brazil at Bahia, he vainly tried to find the coveted Brazil nut (*Bertholletia excelsa*).

Amongst the plants that are found in gardens today, thanks to Don, are the witch hazel *Hamamelis virginiana*, the columbine *Aquilegia canadensis* and kalmias.

A favourite climbing plant for walls and patios is the fremontia or flannel bush (*Fremontodendron* spp.) with its marvellous yellow flowers. It was originally found in Baja California and named after Major General J.C. Frémont (1813-90), who was an explorer and amateur botanist. Another plant originally found in California and named after another botanist was the tree anemone *Carpenteria californica*, named after a doctor from Lousiana, Professor W.M. Carpenter (1811-48).

THE ADVANCE OF SCIENCE

As well as propagating the new introductions, many botanists and horticulturalists of the period were experimenting with hybridization. One of the first people to treat horticulture as a practical science was Thomas Andrew Knight

Below: *The body of David Douglas being lifted out of the bull-trap, from Peter Parley's Tales about Plants (1839).*

Penstemon campanulatus *belongs to a group of 250 species of penstemons which occur in north and central America. Penstemons are popular border plants with tubular flowers in pink, red, mauve and white colours. They belong to the figwort family.*

Above: *Gregor Mendel (1822-84).*

Left: *Douglas fir abounds in the original coastal forest which was conserved in 1888 as Stanley Park, in Vancouver, British Columbia. Stanley Park is bordered on three sides by the Pacific Ocean and the forest, pools and lagoons are a refuge for a rich variety of wildlife.*

(1759-1838), who was President of the Horticultural Society for 27 years. He conducted experiments in hybridization, studying the relative influence of male and female parents and the effect of stocks on their scions in fruit-tree grafting. Most of his papers were subsequently lost, but his work foreshadowed that of the father of genetics, Gregor Mendel (1822-84), who was to have a profound effect on our understanding of genetics and inheritance.

Mendel was the prelate of the monastery at Brunn, (modern Brno), in the central region of Czechoslovakia called Moravia (not, as is frequently misquoted, an abbot living in Austria). He was a keen gardener, who prided himself on his orchard fruit, grapes and wild flowers and regularly exhibited his produce at local flower shows. His experiments with crossing different types of peas led him to propose his *Laws of Mendelian Genetics*, as we now know them. In his garden he raised peas with different characteristics such as smooth or wrinkled skins, tall or short plants, and meticulously cross-pollinated them by hand. By working out which characteristics and what proportions of these appeared in the following generations, he set the basis for the study of genetics. These simple experiments were carried out in a small garden and, indeed, similar studies could be repeated by anyone who has the patience to record meticulous observations.

Mendel wrote up his work in 1866 but it was not until 1900 that its significance became widely known, when it could be seen that it supported Charles Darwin's theory of natural selection. As a good naturalist-gardener Mendel made careful sketches and notes of all that he did, but for 35 years the evidence remained sitting in the monastery library unread by the outside world.

THE
RHODODENDRON
REVOLUTION

There are now over 800 species of rhododendron known today, of which at least 500 species are grown in British gardens. Many of the species have come from the Himalayas, especially around Sikkim and Tibet, thanks to one British collector who literally risked his life in attacks from local inhabitants intent on protecting their country from foreigners. This was Joseph Hooker (1817-1911), son of William Hooker, who was Director of Kew Gardens, a position that Joseph eventually took over.

Around Darjeeling in 1848 Joseph discovered several species of rhododendron, including epiphytic species hanging down from trees (for example *Rhododendron dalhousiae*), and one species 12 m (40 ft) tall (*R. grande*). Altogether some 34 species of rhododendron were collected by Hooker on his expeditions. In Nepal he found alpine species such as *R. anthopogon* with scented leaves. One plant which is named after him is the forget-me-not, *Myosotis hookeri*. He was also responsible for introducing the delightful Himalayan cowslip, *Primula sikkimensis*.

Whilst in the mountains on a precipitous ledge, Hooker experienced the frightening "Spectre of the Brocken", as he called it, when he was confronted by his own outline, complete with halo, standing in the mist a few metres away from him. Joseph Hooker wrote *The Rhododendrons of Sikkim-Himalaya* in 1849, in which his father stated that with the exception of the rose (the "Queen of Flowers"), no other plants had excited so much attention in Europe as the

Sir Joseph Hooker (1817-1911) collecting plants in the Sikkim-Himalaya. During his celebrated Himalayan expedition (1847-51), Hooker found many new species of rhododendron.

rhododendrons. Joseph Hooker increased the number of rhododendron species known in gardens from 19 to 50 at that time. Many of the Sikkim rhododendrons grown in gardens today come from seeds gathered by Hooker in this extraordinary area; there is a valley 80 x 65 km (56 x 40 miles) which contains no less than 30 native species of rhododendron.

Gardening in Victorian times was considerably influenced by plantings of these introduced rhododendrons; well-established species and an increasing range of new ones. Later in the century both Gertrude Jekyll (1843-1932) and William Robinson (1838-1935) had rhododendrons growing wild in their woods, and suggested interplanting with them and moving seedlings to establish clumps elsewhere. The commonest species, then as now, was *R. ponticum*, a native of the region around the Black Sea, which had been introduced to England in 1763. Earlier than this John Tradescant had cultivated *R. hirsutum* from the Alps in 1656. *R. ponticum's* purple flowers are familiar sights in gardens and around lakes, on acid soils. In fact naturalists and conservationists really don't like *ponticum*, because it naturalizes itself by seed and tends to take over in woods to the detriment of native species, and it is difficult to eradicate. And the wildlife potential of rhododendron is quite poor; it attracts only a few gaudily coloured leaf-hoppers (tiny insects related to shield-bugs and aphids) in summer and provides nesting sites for tree sparrows (*Passer montanus*) in spring.

Rhododendron *"Lady Chamberlain"*
First raised in 1930

Rhododendron williamsianum
Introduced 1908

Rhododendron racemosum
Introduced 1889

Rhododendron luteum
Introduced 1793

Rhododendron wightii
Introduced by Joseph Hooker 1849

Rhododendron dauricum
In cultivation 1780

Left: *Charles and Emma Darwin, painted at Down House, Kent.*

Now restricted to wilder areas of the Continent, the military orchid (Orchis militaris, below left) has a formidable spike of flowers. Each flower appears to be blowing a trumpet, hence its "military" or "soldier" name. Honey bees and butterflies such as this speckled wood (Pararge aegeria, below right) visit orchids like this but they must beware of the predatory praying mantis and spiders which lurk in the flowers.

Mendel was very keen on fuchsias and became friends with the fuchsia grower, N. Twrdy. Indeed, he adopted a fuchsia as his emblem, the "Mendel Fuchsia", which Twrdy described as "a seedling from *Fuchsia monstrosa*, very large, pale-blue shading into violet, luxuriant, regular structure, sepals light, very beautiful, blooms early".

Like all good naturalists Mendel had wilder areas in his garden – he eventually developed one side of the nearby mountain with tree forage crops for his bees, thus combining customary monastic duty with utility.

Probably no naturalist has had a more profound effect on scientific thought than Charles Darwin (1809-82) with his revolutionary theories of evolution, expressed in his book *Origin of Species*, which rocked the scientific world when it was published in 1859. Comfortably off with private means (he was the grandson of Josiah Wedgwood, founder of the famous pottery), Darwin had a fine house but a relatively small and formal garden which contained several specimen trees, including a black mulberry (*Morus nigra*) and holm oak (*Quercus ilex*). He was accustomed to walk along the local chalky Downs to study the splendid orchids growing on his favourite "musk orchid bank" (*Herminium monorchis*). In the *Origin of Species* he wrote:

> "He who will carefully examine the flowers of orchids for himself will not deny the existence of the above series of gradations – from a mass of pollen-grains merely tied together by threads, with the stigma differing but little from that of an ordinary flower, to a highly complex pollinium, admirably adapted for transport by insects."

After the publication of the *Origin of Species* Darwin was ridiculed in the press for his controversial theories and became very much a recluse at home, where he was able to enjoy his garden.

The garden did have its wilderness area, a small beech-wood (*Fagus sylvatica*) carpeted in English bluebells (*Endymion non-scriptus*) in the spring, which provided him with a pleasant woodland walk. This is "The Long Walk" with a boundary hedgerow where songbirds nest and wild flowers blossom. The nightingale (*Luscinia megarhynchos*) would sing in these woods too, and the cuckoo (*Cuculus canorus*) call. Speckled wood butterflies (*Pararge aegeria*) would have flown from one area of dappled sunlight to the next. All this can be seen, since the garden and house are open to the public today.

It was in this garden and the wilder area that Darwin drew upon the sights and sounds of nature for his inspiration. He also used the garden for some of his experiments. Visitors today can still see the "worm stone" – a circular stone set in the lawn – that Darwin thought would disappear in time with the continual turn-over of soil. From his desk he would use a theodolite to measure the rate of sinking of the stone. Not all his experiments worked, but he was the first to write a comprehensive book on earthworm biology, which remains a definitive work.

In the autumn of his life Darwin enjoyed the company of several grandchildren – one can almost imagine the tea parties on the lawn – and in true scientific style he used them for one of his experiments. Darwin had noticed that bumble bees have curious "buzzing spots" at the base of large trees or brambles (*Rubus* spp.), and that each year they were always in the same place. He also noticed that bumble bees will suddenly disappear in a hedgerow, only to reappear several metres away. What was the purpose of this? To find out, he set out a string of grandchildren *inside* a hedgerow, within calling distance of each other, and instructed them to let each other know each time a bumble bee passed along its length. By this means Darwin was able to plot the circular movement of bumble bees around the garden and record all the buzzing spots. This patrolling behaviour of bumble bees can be seen in many gardens during the summer; the buzzing spots are chosen by different bees each year and are possibly used as places where scents are deposited.

Living not far from Darwin was Sir John Lubbock (1834-1913), a typical Victorian naturalist who was a little eccentric. He had a distinguished career working in London for most of his life for the London Council and banks (he introduced Bank holidays). For ten years he was the Member of Parliament for Maidstone in Kent, and he was also a proficient archaeologist best remembered for his saving of the Avebury ring.

Lubbock kept a pet wasp which he took to scientific meetings, and invented the glass-sided box, the "Lubbock nest" for looking at ants (two of his ants lived for 14 and 15 years) and he taught his dog to read. He became Darwin's assistant and illustrated some of Darwin's books. He performed various experiments with ants, which proved that they lay scent trails and that they can recognize each other.

In 1885 Lubbock published *Ants, Bees and Wasps*, which contained a lot of experimental work done on this order of insects. He must have been very industrious since he says in his book, "I have kept in captivity about half of our British species of ants, as well as a considerable number of foreign forms, and for the last few years have generally had from thirty to forty communities under observation." These insect societies were kept up on stands with little moats around them to keep them from straying. He describes work carried out by a German friend who encouraged his ants to come from the garden and feed on a sugary solution left on the window sill.

THE
INSECT MAN

Another naturalist fascinated with the microcosmic world of the insect was the Frenchman Jean Henri Fabre (1823-1915). A schoolmaster in Orange, Provence, his garden was small and very informal. He liked to keep it as a sort of wilderness, which is exactly how it is today, peaceful and restful with an excellent unkempt nature. There is a little pond which encourages amphibians and dragonflies; droves of honeybees suck up water at a damp watercourse; the curious hives for solitary bees adorn the garden walls; hedgerows blossom with viburnums, beds with Provençal herbs or native wild plants such as spurges (*Euphorbia* spp.) and cistuses, whilst numerous pots around the ochre-coloured house contain lilies, pelargoniums (popularly called geraniums), sedums (known as ice plants, because they are cold to the touch) and a woody South American lantana for the butterflies. There is no doubt that Fabre encouraged all sorts of wildlife into his garden.

He was fascinated with the digging powers of dung beetles (*Geotrupes* spp.) and the way in which some solitary bees lay their eggs in hollow tubes, such as old

Jean Henri Fabre (1823-1915), photographed in 1913. In his "rampant wild garden . . . even the smallest things appeared mysterious".

bamboo tubes. He constructed special hives which were immediately popular with the local bees. It was Fabre who discovered through simple observation and experiment that the red osmia bee (*Osmia rufa*) lays first of all female-determined eggs at the base of a hole (since they take the longest to develop) and male-determined bees at the front.

Typical of a naturalist of his time Fabre was interested in just about everything, from fossils to flies. His study is a Dickensian picture of haphazard collecting, of herbarium specimens, bell bars, beetles and butterflies. Fabre, widely known as the "insect-man", was a prodigious writer who produced almost 100 books before he died in 1915. He also painted most of the commoner species of fungi of the region, which can be seen today in the museum of the house he lived in.

Jean Henri Fabre's most celebrated book was a ten-volume treatise on insects, entitled *Souvenires Entomologique*, published between 1879-1907. This was widely acclaimed, especially by the Institute of France, and parts have been translated into a dozen languages.

Right: Modern naturalists can provide for the needs of wildlife just as J.H. Fabre did for his red osmia bees. He fitted pieces of hollow canes in a "hive" to give the bees extra space for reproduction, and their populations soared. Securing a few canes under a brick would have the same result. In the wild the bees would normally find old canes or cracks under roof tiles.

Right: A watercolour study of butterflies by Fabre's contemporary, the celebrated British naturalist Philip Gosse (1810-88).

ART IN NATURE

The colourful Provence that Jean Henri Fabre lived in was the same environment that inspired the Impressionist painters, such as Claude Monet (1840-1926). They lived in an idyllic countryside set in flowers. There are still wild corners of Provence that glow with the scarlet of corn poppy (*Papaver rhoeas*) and pheasant's eye (*Adonis aestivalis*), or the yellows of corn marigold (*Chrysanthemum segetum*) and hawkweeds (*Hieracium* spp.) or the blues and purples of cornflowers (*Centaurea cyanus*), the tall blue chicory (*Cichorium intybus*) and tufted vetch (*Vicia cracca*).

Impressionist artists such as Monet himself, Paul Cézanne (1839-1906), Edgar Degas (1834-1917), and Alfred Sisley (1839-99) aimed at capturing the mood of the countryside. This was most evident in Monet's famous series of water lily paintings – twelve very large pictures under the theme of *Le Bassin aux Nymphaeas* – which captured the light and dark moods of the water. According to the Encyclopedia Britannica, this was an "unprecedented, unclassifiable, vast cyclic poem of water, flowers, leaves and light".

Monet found no better place to pursue his interests than in the garden he created at Giverny, west of Paris. He formed a large pond from the adjacent stream, fringed it with weeping willows (*Salix babylonica*) and planted it with water lilies. The serenity, tranquility and moodiness of Monet's water lily pond is enjoyed by tens of thousands of visitors each year, now that his house and newly revived garden are open to the public. Giverny is becoming a French "Sissinghurst", a place of botanic pilgrimage. The gardens are laid out as rows of herbaceous beds in true English style, lively with the reds, blues and yellows of lilies, poppies, salvias, phloxes and campanulas, with brilliant standard roses cascading in blossom. Some of the pink-coloured roses set off the pink rendering of Monet's modest house.

THE NATURAL STYLE

It is sometimes said that the typically English herbaceous border was the invention of William Robinson (1838-1935), the garden lover whose influence dominated the latter half of the nineteenth century and set the pattern for the twentieth. In fact herbaceous borders had been used as early as the 1830s. Nevertheless Robinson, and his contemporary Gertrude Jekyll (1843-1932), were certainly responsible for changing the face of British gardening at a time when formality had returned in force and the mid-century fashion for beds of geometric design planted with colourful annuals and terrace gardens with plant-filled parterres predominated. Robinson deplored what he termed "pastry-work gardening", preferring the natural look and introducing wherever possible foreign plants into an English landscape.

He and Gertrude Jekyll had much in common: they

were of a similar age – Robinson was five years older than Miss Jekyll and lived eight years longer, reaching a fine old age of 97. Both gardened in the south of England, and both liked "wild" gardens. They also both wrote popular books about gardening.

William Robinson was Irish and was initially employed as an apprentice gardener at Curraghmore in County Waterford, south-east Ireland. He then moved to the Royal Botanic Society's garden at Regent's Park, where he soon became curator and travelled around Britain "from the orchid-flecked meadows of Bucks to the tumbled down undercliffs on the Essex coast, untroubled by the plough". He visited York and was amazed by the tropical plants being grown in James Backhouse's greenhouses. Robinson also travelled in the Alps and visited several French gardens. His appreciation of natural habitats and of wild flowers growing in profusion in far-off places inspired the wild-flower gardening themes he would later develop. It is not generally known that Robinson became a wheelchair invalid in 1909 following a fall outside his local church, in which he damaged his spine. In his later years he could not do any gardening himself, and he had a caterpillar tracked Citroën half-truck specially made so that he could be taken cross-country around his estate in his wheelchair.

In 1884 William Robinson came to live at the old sixteenth-century manor house of Gravetye, set in 400 ha (988 acres) of wooded West Sussex countryside. It is now a luxury hotel where the extensive gardens have been carefully restored by the present management, following the basic plan designed by Robinson. Here he created his fine English garden that so many would try to copy; a terraced garden, now dominated by cedars and pines, a vast wind-break of conifers against the prevailing westerly winds, a long lawn set between drifts of azaleas on ground rising up from the house, and an enormous oval walled kitchen garden – perhaps a design copied from Regent's Park.

Far left: *Rose bushes border one of the long paths through the garden at Giverny.*

Left: *Monet's water garden, the inspiration for so many of his paintings.*

Above: *Monet, photographed while painting his cycle of water-lily paintings.*

Right: *Shrouded behind the façade of Chinese wisteria (Wisteria sinensis), William Robinson's home, Gravetye Manor, lies in wooded countryside, much of which Robinson planted. In his earlier years, Robinson was a keen forester, gardener and travel writer, and twentieth-century gardeners owe much to his influence.*

Below: *The guelder rose (Viburnum opulus) with autumn fruits.*

Right: *Great gardeners plan for vistas they often never see, but William Robinson, almost a centenarian, lived long enough to appreciate the maturing of his plantings. The intermixture of azaleas, rhododendrons and Scots pine (Pinus sylvestris) harmonizes perfectly despite the different origins of the plants. Robinson's genius for interplanting different species is seen throughout his gardens, which have been lovingly preserved.*

The walls and house are typically obscured in Virginia creeper, the porch is covered with house-leeks (*Sempervivum* spp.) and the old English oaks are garlanded in climbing hydrangea (*Hydrangea petiolaris*). The wild woods of Robinson's day are a riot of daffodils and red camellias in the spring (recalling the sub-tropical gardens of Abbotsbury in Dorset) and Portugal laurel (*Prunus lusitanica*). The lake, which he created specially, fringed at one end by bamboos, sets off the alpine meadow which lies on the hill up to the house. Robinson's collecting trip to the Alps had influenced his planting and garden design. The east garden is a mass of spectacular azaleas and rhododendrons contrasting with the tall Scots pine.

Between 1889 and 1890 Robinson had planted 120,000 trees which comprised 1,000 silver maples (*Acer saccharinum*), 100 *Liquidambar styraciflua*, 5,000 hollies (*Ilex aquifolium*) and 1,000 cedars of Lebanon (*Cedrus libani*). Today his trees have matured and the estate lies deep in forestry. It was fitting that he gave the management of the forests to the Forestry Commission.

SETTING NEW TRENDS

Perhaps Robinson's greatest achievement was in conveying his experiences of gardening to the general public through his writings. He had started out as a gardening correspondent after leaving Regent's Park and had covered the Paris Exhibition of 1867 for *The Times*, *The Field* and *The Gardener's Chronicle*. In 1871 he founded *The Garden* magazine and included contributions from friends in America, where he had just visited. Miss Jekyll helped with botanical illustrations but she too soon started writing. In 1879 Robinson launched the magazine *Gardening Illustrated* which also became popular. Soon Robinson was producing books which brought him considerable wealth. His first best-seller was *The English Flower Garden*, published in 1883, but his first book was *The Wild Garden* in 1870. He also published a periodical of fine watercolour paintings in 1903-05 called *Flora and Sylva* and another on clematis; it was recognized at the time that he had at Gravetye Manor the best collection of clematis in Europe.

Charles Darwin's controversial views on natural selection were still fresh in everyone's minds following publication of his *Origin of Species* in 1859, and Robinson was rather sceptical about the "survival of the fittest" theory. This, of course, could be relevant to any "wild garden" where species have to fend for themselves. Accordingly, he cast bulbs about in the woods, without digging them in, to see whether the fittest would survive: perhaps in defiance of Darwin's theories. Robinson liked to have plenty of exotic plants in his borders, which he called "mixed borders". He considered that a general herbaceous border should be 2.7 to 4.5 m (9 to 15 ft) wide and that particular attention should be given to heights of plants, with natural settings and continuous colour all year.

Like most gardeners Robinson had his plant preferences, and not all the exotics took his fancy. He loved golden rod (*Solidago* spp.) and Michaelmas daisies (*Aster* spp.) but did not care for giant redwoods: "The passion for the exotic is so universal that our own finest plants are never planted, while money is thrown away like chaff for worthless exotic trees like the American Wellingtonia (*Sequoiadendron giganteum*)." This must have been a dislike of the particular species, since Robinson is very careful to define what he means by a "wild" garden in the introduction to his book *The Wild Garden*, applying it essentially to the placing of perfectly hardy exotic plants under conditions where they will thrive without further care. It has nothing to do with the old idea of the "Wilderness".

A typical fine native plant much neglected then was the guelder rose *Viburnum opulus*, not even found in the Waterer's nurseries at Oxford at the time (Anthony Waterer was a friend of Robinson); it is, however, a firm favourite today. Some conflicting attitudes can be detected in Robinson's opinions: if he did not like exotics, why then did he plant exotic trees in his grounds? Why too did he have formal beds of roses outside his house – and critics drew attention to this – when he advocated "wild gardens"?

Both William Robinson and Gertrude Jekyll had wild woods where great specialities were the new North American plants, wood lilies (*Trillium* spp.), false Solomon's seal *Smilacina racemosa* and the North American fern or hay-scented fern *Dennstaedtia punctilobula*, or the delicate blue anemone from the Appenines in Italy, the British native pasque flower (*Pulsatilla vulgaris*), or the pheasant's eye (*Adonis aestivalis*). "Take a spreading old summer-leafing tree," said Robinson, "and scatter a few tufts of the winter aconite (*Eranthis hyemalis*) beneath it, and leave them alone" – this was the way he liked to garden. He liked the colour contrasts and the unusual: the enormous leaves of *Gunnera* – too big for present-day small gardens – or Virginia creeper (*Parthenocissus* spp.) threading up through weeping willows (*Salix babylonica*), or white clematis contrasting with dark yew, or "a beautiful accident" of *Myrrhis odorata* and white harebells (*Campanula* spp.).

Though he didn't like rabbits in the garden, Robinson showed a keen interest in the inter-relationships of wildlife, observing that hares don't do too well in rabbit-rich areas, rabbits keep the grass down and exclude pheasants, which are frequent diggers in the garden; pheasants prefer holly in which to roost and rabbits do gardeners a favour by eating holly seedlings. Although there are plenty of plants which have rabbit-proof bark because there are nauseous chemicals present – elder (*Sambacus nigra*) for instance, or American azaleas – rabbits did eat the bark of Oregon grape (*Mahonia aquifolium*), yew (*Taxus baccata*) and even perwinkle (*Vinca* spp.) in hard winters in Robinson's garden.

GERTRUDE JEKYLL

No one supported the naturalistic approach to gardening more enthusiastically than Gertrude Jekyll, though she recognized the need to control it. Remembered mostly for her garden designs with Sir Edwin Lutyens, she is less well known for the way in which her gardens reflected simple elements of the countryside – a genuine natural approach. Born in 1843, she lived to 89, but her failing eyesight meant that eventually she could only appreciate the subtle perfumes and textures of the plants in her garden at Munstead, in Surrey.

Many of Miss Jekyll's original ideas for garden design have been lost in gardens today, which in comparison seem almost stereotyped and uninteresting. She incorporated native trees and shrubs into most of her gardens. Starting with a 4 ha (10 acre) pine wood recently felled, she selected only those trees which naturally exploited the cleared land well, such as holly (*Ilex aquifolium*), mountain ash (*Sorbus aucuparia*), silver birch (*Betula pendula*), oak (*Quercus* spp.), beech (*Fagus* spp.) and yew (*Taxus baccata*). She was also an artist and photographer and has left us a legacy of pictures of her carefully designed gardens which were sheltered by the trees, or by dark yew hedges which helped to contrast and set off the colours of low-growing plants. She preferred to call her herbaceous borders "drifts", from the way in which drifts of colour blended in with each other, and she was keen on hanging garlands of clematis, though she did not have the extensive use of the 250 varieties of clematis known today. There were colourful gardens for all seasons for her aim was to achieve colour all the year round. Some believed it might be cheating to lift a pot of brightly coloured annuals and bed them into the herbaceous border for good effect, but Miss Jekyll was an expert at such things.

The species she chose for the garden reflected the greatly increased choice available to gardeners towards the end of the century, particularly American species such as the American brambles *Rubus parviflorus* and *R. odoratus*, the North American ginger (*Asarum virginianum*), and *Gaultheria*

Gertrude Jekyll (1843-1932), painted by Sir William Nicholson in 1920. She began to design gardens in the 1880s.

shrub and Monterey cypress (*Cupressus macrocarpa*). Her woodland walks were planted in a natural fashion with rhododendron (*R. ponticum*), patches of native lily of the valley (*Convallaria majalis*), foxgloves (*Digitalis purpurea*), male ferns (*Dryopteris filix-mas*) and royal ferns (*Osmunda regalis*), as well as the much neglected North American *Amelanchier*. She had an impressive primrose (*Primula* spp.) garden which took thirty years to select and establish the prolific-flowering stock. Her specially bred strains of plants would soon carry the familiar "Munstead" or "Jekyll" name: honesty *Lunaria annua "Munstead"*, love-in-the-mist (*Nigella damascena*), columbines (*Aquilegia* spp.), polyanthus and the variety of greater periwinkle *Vinca major "Jekyll's White"*.

Gertrude Jekyll suggested planting in the orchard alongside apples and pears native British trees such as the damson and bullace – both species of *Prunus* – crab apples and service trees, all of which would supply extra wild fruits for the birds and insects. Both the service tree (a wild *Sorbus* species) and wild crabs have since declined alarmingly in Britain; where they have been felled they have never been replaced. The service tree's other name of chequer tree – after its light and dark bark – gives rise to the name of many English pubs called "The Chequers". Fruit trees such as medlars (*Mespilus germanica*), quinces (*Cydonia oblonga*) and mulberry (*Morus* spp.) could be interspersed with wild species, such as mountain ash, wild cherry, blackthorn, whitebeam (*Sorbus aria*), holly and amelanchier (*Amelanchier laevis*), which, as she explained, catered for "the birds' and botanists' point of view": fruits and seeds for the birds, and a range of trees and wild plants in the long grass of the orchard to interest plant lovers.

Miss Jekyll's enthusiasm for gardening inspired thousands of amateur gardeners throughout the Old World and the New. As she declared in *A Gardener's Testament* in *Country Life* (1937):

"After all, what is a garden for?
It is for 'delight', for 'sweet solace', for 'the purest of all human pleasures;
the greatest refreshment of the spirits of men';
it is to promote 'jucunditie of minde';
it is to 'call home over-wearied spirits'. So say the old writers,
and we cannot amend their words, which will stand as long as there are gardens
on earth and people to love them."

Above: *Munstead Wood,
photographed by
Gertrude Jekyll in 1900.*

Right: *A drawing of
Gertrude Jekyll by
Sir Edwin Lutyens (c. 1896).*

Soon after the beginning of the century Gertrude Jekyll started to contribute regularly to *The Garden* and *Country Life* magazines on gardening matters, and went on to write fourteen popular books on gardening, including *Home and Garden, Gardens for Small Country Houses* and *Wood and Garden*. As a designer of gardens she was in great demand and contributed ideas for at least 300 gardens. These included 100 gardens which she designed with her neighbour and business partner Sir Edwin Lutyens (1869-1944), an architect who clearly had a feeling for the natural disposition of plants in towns and cottage gardens. He designed the house she built in 1896, Munstead Wood, and shared the planning of the garden.

Lutyens was considerably influenced by the American idea of green Garden Cities and his work both in Britain and India reflected this. An example can be seen in the garden suburb of Hampstead, North London.

ACROSS THE ATLANTIC

The American scheme of "Garden Cities" was set up by A.T. Stewart in 1869 to integrate green areas into the urban scene with parks, avenues of trees and green squares. The first one was at Long Island, New York, and the idea was soon adopted in Europe. The first in England was Letchworth (1899) followed closely by Welwyn Garden City (1903). Green areas are now designed into most cities, not only as a breathing space for people but as a refuge for urban wildlife. Another American idea which has been adopted throughout the western world is the "Garden Centre". The idea was taken up in Australia before it arrived in Europe in the early 1900s.

An effort was made to turn New York green with the creation of Central Park, started in 1856. This was the brainchild of Frederick Law Olmsted (1822-1903) and the Frenchman Calvert Vaux, whose plan won the hotly fought competition. Central Park, with its copious green expanses, was the first attempt in America to integrate nature into a public park. Olmsted went on to design and influence the building of numerous parks such as Prospect Park, Brooklyn; South Park, Chicago; the Capitol Grounds, Washington; Stanford University, California; Niagara Park and Mt Royal Park in Montreal, Canada. Bronx Park, New York, is noted for its botanical and zoological exhibitions, and other "green" areas are Riverside Park and Green Park.

The famous American artist-naturalist, John James Audubon (1785-1851), noted for his remarkable figures of birds, is remembered in New York by Audubon Park, where he used to live. Audubon was born in Haiti, brought up in France and was intensely interested in birds. He made a lasting contribution to ornithology in America through his *Birds of America*, published between 1827 and 1838.

American gardens had come a long way since the days of the early settlers. Descriptions of Californian gardens at this time speak of heliotrope hedges 5 m (16 ft) tall, geraniums climbing to the second storey of houses, a night-flowering Peruvian apple cactus (*Cereus peruvianus*) halfway over a house and acres of calla lilies (*Calla indica*). A false acacia (*Robinia pseudoacacia*) would grow a 15 cm (6 in) diameter trunk in three years from sowing; a eucalyptus would grow to 25 m (82 ft) in eight years.

AMERICAN PLANTS
INTRODUCED IN THE NINETEENTH CENTURY
(date of entry into England supplied where known)

American arrowhead
(*Sagittaria rigida*) 1822

Columbine (*Aquilegia canadensis*)

Evening primroses
(*Oenothera* spp.)

Flannel bush
(*Fremontodendron californicum*)

Flannel bush
(*Fremontodendron mexicana*)

Halectroides
(*Halectroides pennsylvanica*)

Hepatica (*Hepatica americana*)

Monkey flower
(*Mimulus guttatus*) 1812

Evening primrose

Old woman
(*Artemisia stellerana*)

Oregon grape
(*Mahonia aquifolium*) 1823

Pink wood sorrel
(*Oxalis* spp.) 1870

San Diego lilac
(*Ceanothus cyaneus*)

Snowberry
(*Symphoricarpos* spp.) 1817

Tree anemone
(*Carpenteria californica*) 1812

Yellow adders-tongue
(*Erythronium americanum*)

In the second half of the nineteenth century there were several interesting gardens to visit in California. Johann Georg Lehrmann (1792-1860) created a fantastic "Garden of Paradise" in Los Angeles, complete with "Garden of Eden", a cross between jungleland and rose gardens. At Hollywood Edward Sturtevant (1848-98) was an expert at water lilies and had a giant Royal water-lily (*Victoria amazonica*) growing successfully in the 1890s, with its huge, saucer-shaped 2 m (6 ft) diameter floating leaves.

There was only one outstanding garden in San Diego at the turn of the present century and that was the nursery of Kate Olivia Sessions (1851-1940). She created a colourful garden from drought-resistant Californian native species like the flannel bush and the San Diego lilac (*Ceanothus cyaneus*), and blended these with her imported acacias from Australia and silver trees (*Leucadendron argenteum*) from South Africa.

Another local plant was the Californian tree poppy or Matilija poppy (*Romneya coulteri*), whose common name recalls a famous Indian chief, Matilija, and whose Latin name commemorates a local doctor-botanist, Dr Coulter.

Above: *Butchart Gardens, near Victoria, are among the most celebrated gardens in British Columbia. They were established in 1904 to beautify a local quarry and have subsequently been expanded to include a Japanese and an Italian Garden.*

Right: *A bird's eye view of Central Park, New York, from the south, by John Bachmann (1863).*

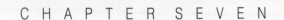

CHAPTER SEVEN

THE
NATURALIST'S GARDEN TODAY

A new enthusiasm for "wild" gardens and gardening for wildlife has arisen this century. Many gardens now feature a special "wilderness" area, in which plants are encouraged to mix freely and attract all kinds of different insects and mammals. The traditional dividing line between flowers and weeds is becoming blurred. As wild flowers are increasingly threatened with extinction in their native habitats, more people are introducing them into their gardens. One attractive way of conserving endangered species of wild plants is to create a "wild" lawn, where traditional hedgerow flowers mingle with mixed long grasses. By careful planting, colour and interest can be maintained throughout the year.

Interesting new species of plants are still being discovered around the world. Some of the most important contributions to present day gardens have been made by naturalists and botanists of the present century, who very often risked their lives to collect exotic plants growing in remote regions.

Springtime in the cherry tree walk
at Sutton Place, Surrey.

The movement in favour of naturalistic gardening headed by William Robinson at the end of the nineteenth century did not go unchallenged. The publication in 1892 of *The Formal Garden in England*, by Reginald Blomfield and F. Inigo Thomas, presented a strong case for the revival of formalism in garden design. Gertrude Jekyll herself, a staunch supporter of Robinson's ideas, learned to modify her approach in her collaboration with the architect Edwin Lutyens, adapting plants and colour schemes to blend skilfully with garden layouts that incorporated many more formal gardens.

In the end, it is perhaps more than anyone else Gertrude Jekyll's influence that has permeated garden development in our own century, bringing together the best of styles inherited from the past in a happy compromise, a blend between formal and informal, the peak of man-made art with the glories of the plant world. Her genius was the ability to select exactly the right balance of colour, form and texture to match new architectural schemes, to meet the search for beauty in its natural form and to deal with the demands of a changing world.

And indeed the world was changing fast. The days of the great estates were numbered: wealthy patrons were a dwindling race. Already the introduction of estate duty in 1894 had affected the balance of riches, and there was appreciably less money to be spent on the embellishment of large gardens. The first World War destroyed for ever the established order; labour became expensive as money became short. Another generation of gardeners emerged, keen amateurs with their 27 x 9 m (90 x 30 ft) plots on the housing estates that grew like a rash round all the big towns between the wars. They gardened for pleasure, doing their own work, and they were hungry for information. This was furnished by a proliferation of gardening books and magazines that were published – and still are being produced – to satisfy the growing demand.

THE COTTAGE GARDEN

The neat suburban garden of the twentieth century, with its trimmed hedges and bedding plants, was in quite a different category from the old cottage garden which enjoyed special limelight at the turn of the century in Gertrude Jekyll's writings. Hers was a romanticized concept, however, more closely related to a reduced version of the herbaceous border of a big estate than the truly traditional "cottage" garden. This was a far more practical affair, a means of survival for the rural poor, where they could grow vegetables and fruit to support themselves and supplement an otherwise restricted diet. Though flowers were often grown they were a luxury and consisted mostly of traditional kinds, such as roses and marigolds, cornflowers, sunflowers and hollyhocks. The "cottage gardens" she advocated were more likely to be found attached to the houses of the better-off – in *Home and Garden* (1900) Miss Jekyll refers to her own house as little larger than a cottage.

The romanticized view of the cottage garden was fostered by the paintings of such artists as Helen Allingham, who at one time was an illustrator for the novelist Thomas Hardy. She devoted her time to painting cottages and their gardens, especially in the south of England.

Far left: Helen Allingham's paintings of rural England established a romantic image of cottage gardens that remains very popular.

Left: Delphiniums and rambling roses frame this farmhouse in Shamley Green, Surrey, in typical "cottage garden" style.

The country cottages that Helen Allingham painted from life are as natural looking, colourful and quaint as one could ever imagine an English home to be. They were idealized pictures of working houses, with bonneted women and children, chickens and ducks; picturesque views of streams, mills and tiny bridges, waysides full of wild flowers, colourful herbaceous borders, rambling roses covering wattle and daub walls, reaching to the thatched or tiled roofs. Tall elms and poplars stand in the fields and along the lanes. Her paintings seem to show perpetual spring and summer, always a riot of colour. Sticky mud and dismal winter scenes are not depicted.

The wildness of the gardens surrounding the cottages are particularly striking. The colours of the tall hollyhocks, sunflowers, white lilies, delphiniums, old roses, lilac, snapdragons and cornflowers sometimes rubbed shoulders with huge cabbages or fruit trees. These were times of very informal gardens and earth paths. The rich vegetation suggests a reliance upon staple perennial plants mixed with a few opportunist annuals. The old English herbal plants, such as tansy, yarrow, pansies and lavender all grow together. Beyond the gates and the untidy hedges the waysides are just as colourful. Wild flowers crowd out the laneside grasses making a pattern of colour that people today try to re-create with their "instant meadow" mixtures.

The scenes are reminiscent of Flora Thompson's description in *Lark Rise to Candleford* of a prosperous cottage garden in an Oxfordshire village of the 1880s:

"Near the cottage were fruit trees, then the yew hedge, close and solid as a wall, which sheltered the beehives and enclosed the flower garden. Sally had such flowers, and so many of them, and nearly all of them sweet-scented! Wallflowers and tulips, lavender and sweet william, and pinks and old-world roses with enchanting names...."

SOME OUTSTANDING GARDENS

Reminders of the old-fashioned cottage garden where plants are raised in casual association and allowed to seed themselves can be seen in some of the oustanding gardens of our own times. One of the finest examples is Sissinghurst, creation of Vita Sackville-West (1892-1962). With her husband, Harold Nicolson, she made two gardens, the first between 1915 and 1930 at Long Barn, near Sevenoaks in Kent, and the second at Sissinghurst Castle in Kent between 1930 and 1961. Now managed by the National Trust, Sissinghurst is probably the most visited garden in Britain.

PATCHWORK GARDEN

When Vita Sackville-West took over the Elizabethan manor at Sissinghurst it was exceedingly run-down. She and her husband started from scratch and established a series of walled and hedged gardens, avenues and herb gardens that would delight both botanists and naturalists.

Between 1947 and 1961 she wrote extensively on everyday gardening matters for *The Observer* and did much to popularize gardening, publishing a series of books which included *In Your Garden* (1951) and *Even More for your Garden* (1958).

The charm of Sissinghurst is its natural effect. Vita Sackville-West vigorously opposed the formal tidiness of gardens and encouraged plants to grow wherever their seedlings sprang up, or their boughs overhung the paths. She gardened in a patchwork of walled or yew-hedged compartments which were integrated into what was left of old Elizabethan courtyards. Her husband planned the layout of both Long Barn and Sissinghurst.

One spectacular feature is the white garden planted with white and grey-coloured species set off by the dark foliage of the box hedge. There are *Rosa alba*, the White Rose of York; festoons of the *Rosa filipes*; white almond blossom; grey foliage of Scotch or cotton thistle (*Onopordon acanthium*); willow (*Salix* spp.); white lamb's tongue (*Stachys lanata* "Silver Carpet") and white delphiniums.

Victoria "Vita" Sackville-West (1892-1962) created the splendid gardens at Sissinghurst, Kent, from a wilderness.
Right: *An aerial view of Sissinghurst gardens from the Tudor tower.*

On the walls are cascades of white clematis, and the albino form of the cup-and-saucer plant (*Cobaea scandens*) from Mexico; growing up a pergola is the climbing potato vine (*Solanum jasminoides*). These contrast well with the massed ranks of summer hyacinth (*Galtonia candicans*) planted in front of the dark box hedges.

The herb garden is another major attraction. In design it has hardly changed from the photographs taken there in the 1930s. Embraced by yew hedges, this small herb garden is packed with medicinal species which offer a potted history of herbal medicine in Europe and, at the centre, there is a pot of exquisite red sedums. Some of the more unusual plants grow here, such as the shoo-fly plant (*Nicandra physalodes*) and the real mandrake (*Mandragora officinarum*), not to be confused with the old English name for the red bryony (*Bryonia dioica* – it is said to scream violently if pulled up!).

The white garden at Sissinghurst mixes white, cream, silver and grey plants to superb effect. It has been described as "the most beautiful garden . . . in all of England".

Right: A view through the "white" garden towards Hidcote Manor, Gloucestershire. The garden has been managed by the National Trust since 1948.

Below: Hibiscus rosa-sinensis *var.* cooperi.

Hidcote, too, is an outstanding garden, considered by many to be the finest example of the twentieth century. Created by Major Lawrence Johnston from 1907 onwards, Hidcote Manor was constructed on a cold site, and consists of a series of small compartments protected by hedges behind which many semi-tender and unusual plants such as the Chilean climber, *Tropaeoleum speciosum*, have been successfully established. Like Sissinghurst, the art of Hidcote lies in its apparent naturalness. Aspects have been borrowed from the cottage garden, in the Jekyll tradition, with plants allowed their freedom, and there is a wild area in the valley called the "Wilderness". Major Johnston, who died in 1957, was a knowledgeable plantsman, widely travelled, and the garden contains a number of interesting plants and trees, including a fine variety of hypericum named *Hypericum patulum* "Hidcote" and the "Hidcote" lavender.

Another exponent of the style of gardening developed by Gertrude Jekyll, with whom she has sometimes been compared, was Margery Fish (1892-1969). She converted an abandoned two-acre farmyard at East Lambrook Manor, Somerset, into an old-style cottage garden with 2,000 plant species. With a passion for gardening, she collected variegated and double forms and different cultivars of primrose (she had at least 60, some of which have now become extinct),

Above: *The fish pond at Chartwell, Kent. Sir Winston Churchill enjoyed watching the golden orfes gliding through the water.*

Below: *Such aristocrats as the comma butterfly* (Polygonia c-album) *were regular visitors to the wild flowers at Chartwell.*

and violets. She also experimented with growing hostas and begonias and in hybridizing hellebores. She turned her garden into a typically English cottage garden and her writings – she wrote eight books – encouraged thousands of people to re-establish some of the old favourites among plant species. Popular titles were *Cottage Garden Flowers, Gardening on Clay and Limestone* and *We Made a Garden.* Today, her nursery is commemorated through plants such as *Artemisia* "Lambrook Silver" and visitors can still see Margery Fish's "pudding trees" – her carefully clipped Lawson cypresses (*Chamaecyparis lawsoniana*).

GARDENING FOR WILDLIFE

Winston Churchill (1874-1965) developed a keen interest in natural history and gardening at his country home of Chartwell. Set in an idyllic coombe on the North Downs in Kent and blessed with a regular source of water, Chartwell provided an excuse for Churchill to create pools at different levels (exercising his engineering skills), introduce wildlife and build himself a walled kitchen garden.

The simple but inspiring gardens are dominated by the views over the Weald of Kent and Sussex and the wooded scarps on the Downs. The invasive Victorian rhododendrons on the lawn were removed and the old house renovated. It was Churchill's hope that on his death the National Trust, which now looks after Chartwell, would keep plenty of plants like buddleia and lavender to attract the colourful butterflies that he encouraged.

The lepidopterist, L. Hugh Newman, came to Chartwell in the spring of 1939 to introduce a butterfly colony. After the war, in 1946, Newman's son continued the regular stocking of the gardens with butterflies and between 1,000 and 1,500 were released into the garden each year. The brick summerhouse was converted into a butterfly house – one of the first in England – using the wooden seats as benches on which to rear the caterpillars. Churchill would sit for hours watching the insects hatch and would then liberate them into his colourful garden. Species reared included the peacock butterfly (*Inachis io*), small tortoiseshell (*Aglais urticae*), brimstone (*Gonepteryx rhamni*), comma (*Polygonia c-album*), red admiral (*Vanessa atalanta*), painted lady (*Cynthia cardui*) and the clouded yellow (*Colias croceus*). The black-veined white (*Aporia crataegi*) was imported from the Continent and liberated in the garden; it had become extinct in Britain after 1912 and was something of a curiosity.

In true Konrad Lorenz-style, Churchill had a tame Canada goose which would follow him every time he walked down by the lakes. Lorenz had proved that goslings would accept as their "mother" whoever reared them immediately after hatching. There was a robin (*Erithacus rubecula*) which learned to feed from Churchill's hand, and amongst his other pets at various times were a badger (*Meles meles*), a fox and a rather smelly sheep. He had tons of rocks sent down from Cumberland to create a water garden and he stocked this with golden orfe carp. He would sit at the poolside watching these fish and throw them maggots which were sent regularly from Yorkshire. There were also some famous black swans which were a gift from the Australians. He planted limes (*Tilia* spp.), whose nectar-rich flowers attract thousands of humming bees in early summer.

A living example of wildlife gardening can be seen at Great Dixter in Kent, the home of that connoisseur of gardening matters, Christopher Lloyd (b. 1921). The impressive fifteenth-century manor house was extensively restored by Sir Edwin Lutyens in 1910, who also fashioned its garden. There are magnificent splayed steps and walls at different levels from which can be admired the profusion and juxtaposition of rampant wild plants. The sunken garden is a picture of colour and a bowl of scent, resplendent in spring with plants such as wood anemone (*Anemone nemorosa*), forget-me-not (*Myosotis* spp.), white and purple honesty (*Lunaria annua*), lesser celandines (*Ranunculus ficaria*), the greater periwinkle (*Vinca major*) and wallflowers (*Cheiranthus cheiri*), and there are at least 15 species of grass here. There is one of a surviving pair of mulberry trees overlooking the formal rose garden. This is full of old Bourbons and the expanse of wild orchard is bedecked with fritillaries and narcissi in the spring.

A major feature of Great Dixter is the dark yew hedges, either cut into bird forms or used to divide off small areas including kitchen garden, nursery beds and colourful herbaceous borders. There are 18 of these quaint gardening compartments. The hedges also offer protection from the wind and show off the colour of some lighter flowers with stunning effect.

Lutyens made great use of the old farm buildings in his design and many a wall is hung with mature espalier pears of antique proportions, or rare schizandra. Aubrieta, coton-easter and Canary Island ivy (*Hedera canariensis*) drape the old walls and blackbirds (*Turdus merula*) and thrushes (*Turdus philomelos*) nest in the thick hedges and find juicy worms in the flower beds. Swallows (*Hirundo rustica*) nest in the barns and the collared doves (*Streptopelia decaocto*) recently introduced to Britain flit around the garden.

There is an air of Robinson and Jekyll about Great Dixter, of specially arranged colour mixtures and different plant species growing together with great effect. In *The Mixed Border* (1986) Christopher Lloyd points out the reasons and advantages of having mixed borders: "In nature, plants mix all the time, so why not in the garden?" There are also likely to be fewer attacks from pests and diseases, as insects and disease pathogens cannot move next door to the same species, which they can do easily in, for instance, beds of roses.

Clematis are among Christopher Lloyd's specialist groups and he has mastered the art of getting them to run through shrubs and trees, such as a stunning purple clematis

These giant poppies Papaver orientale "Goliath" *contrast beautifully with the dark yew hedge in the gardens of Great Dixter. A connoisseur of wild flower gardening, Christopher Lloyd has made Great Dixter a mecca for exponents of "wilder" gardens.*

twining through *Pieris* "Forest Flame". His famous long border, 64 m (210 ft) long and 13 m (42 ft) deep, is a riot of colour in the summer with wild roses, giant alliums, delphiniums and salvias, hostas and phloxes; sedums and lady's mantle (*Alchemilla mollis*) creep over the flagstones; colourful annuals and biennials are planted everywhere. This giant herbaceous border is mixed with woody perennials, such as tamarisks, escallonias, magnolias and Dickson's golden elm (*Ulmus angustifolia* "Dicksonii").

Christopher Lloyd did not invent wild flower gardening but he is one of the few to foster it for public display. One of his special creations is the wild lawn – envied by most gardeners and naturalists who strive to have a trouble-free, colourful lawn which won't succumb under long, lank grass. The springtime meadows which surround the timber-framed house are a riot of colour from a host of wild flowers: early purple orchids, purple and white coloured fritillaries, docks (*Rumex* spp.), primroses and primulas and bluebells (*Endymion non-scriptus*). Ordinary daisies and dandelions (*Taraxacum officinalis*), cuckoo flowers, known also as milk maids and lady's smock (*Cardamine pratensis*), wood anemone (*Anemone nemorosa*) and buttercups (*Ranunculus* spp.) also thrive, with cow parsley (*Anthriscus sylvestris*) and various mixed grasses. In the autumn the lawns flower with autumn crocus (*Colchicum autumnale*) and the borders

with the tiny cyclamen (*Cyclamen neapolitanum* now called *C. hederifolium*). To create such an interesting diversity it is actually necessary to put in a lot of work in cutting the grass at particular times of the year.

There is no one quite as renowned for meadow gardening as the naturalist Miriam Rothschild (b. 1907). An international expert on fleas, she is equally at home discussing the mimicry of butterflies or the latest theories in ecology. Her private gardens are a carpet of flowers; in fact it was Dr Rothschild who generated the enormous interest in Britain in growing wild flowers for seed – "the wild flower seed boom".

Starting in 1980 with an acre of cowslips grown for their seed, she now only considers a minimum area of about

Above: *The long border at Great Dixter, East Sussex. Careful planting ensures that it remains colourful for most of the year.*

Left: *Christopher Lloyd's wild meadow, which leads to the house and more formal garden "compartments".*

2 ha (5 acres) as a viable proposition for seed production. The market for wild flower seed grew so quickly in the early 1980s that wild flower gardening on the grand scale is now the only profitable way. Daisy seed (*Bellis perennis*), for instance, still remains a precious commodity for which there will always be a great demand, since it is such a typical "wild" flower and few people have the time, acreage or patience to produce and harvest the fine seed.

Miriam Rothschild gardens on the rich Northamptonshire soil at Ashton, where the village pub is named *The Chequered Skipper* after the rare butterfly (*Carterocephalus palaemon*). Now sadly extinct in England, it used to fly about the Ashton meadows. Around her house, Dr Rothschild scatters wild flower seed in early spring to populate a colourful meadow; early purple and common spotted orchids (*Orchis mascula* and *Dactylorchis maculata* respectively) mingle with campions (*Silene* spp.), corncockles (*Agrostemma githago*) and cornflowers (*Centaurea cyanus*). This is no place for neatly clipped lawns, selective herbicides and fancy flower beds; the old greenhouses, once festooned with grapes, now house tropical butterflies, such as North American monarchs (*Danaus plexippus*), South American heliconids and African and Asian swallow-tails, which feed on passion flowers, milkweed flowers (*Asclepias* spp.) and heliotropes. Even the humble cabbage white butterfly (*Pieris brassicae*) is reared here for experimental purposes. Other wildlife is important too in Miriam Rothschild's garden. Any description would be incomplete without a mention of the pet magpies (*Pica pica*) and owls, the herd of Père David's deer (*Elaphuras davidianus*) grazing the meadow, the flocks of white doves, the semi-wild fox (*Vulpes vulpes*) or, indeed, her beloved Border collie dogs.

One of Miriam Rothschild's latest ventures is marketing seeds of her Holy Land wild flowers through the noted seedsman, John Chambers. Among the species now available, are the Israeli cornflower (*Centaurea cynaroides*), the blue mountain lupin (*Lupinus varius*) and the Palestine campion (*Silene palaestina*).

Dr Rothschild's most widely seen contribution to "wild" gardening is her establishment of a typical medieval corn meadow outside the butterfly centre at Stratford-upon-Avon in 1986. It is jewelled with all the wild flowers of ancient meadows, many of which have now disappeared owing to the use of herbicides, loss of habitats, and the improved mechanical techniques of separating (cleaning) weed seeds from the crop. Such species as corn marigold (*Chrysanthemum segetum*), cornflower (*Centaurea cyanus*), corncockle (the seeds of which used to cause gastroenteritis when ground up with the corn) and the favourite corn poppy (*Papaver rhoeas*) sparkle between the stems of wheat. Among her many other enterprises have been the establishment of wild flower meadows on motorway verges and a private wild flower meadow at Highgrove in Gloucestershire, the country home of H.R.H. The Prince and Princess of Wales.

One of the finest historic houses in Britain, Sutton Place in Surrey, an early sixteenth-century house built for King Henry VIII, now has a modern garden fit for wildlife. Very little remains of the original Tudor and Elizabethan gardens, save the walled kitchen garden. In the Georgian period "Capability" Brown was invited here to make suggestions for landscaping, but was apparently sent away after he suggested pushing aside the avenues of trees. Gertrude Jekyll came to Sutton Place in 1902 to advise on plantings and the yew hedges established by Lady Northcliffe were in accordance with her suggestions.

Today, naturalists enjoy the specially planned wild woods and meadows, the wildfowl and many different wild flowers. Designed by Sir Geoffrey Jellicoe in 1980, it is a complex of small gardens with a pleasant mixture of natural features.

Several different styles of gardening can be seen at Sutton Place, a blend of English gardening history: the classical style with the exhibition of statuary, like the Italian gardens of Hever; the Paradise Garden, a direct reference to some medieval gardens; the small walled or hedged gardens (the East and West Walled Garden), so well mastered at Sissinghurst and Great Dixter, and in the Wild Garden the wild-flower plantings of both Jekyll and Robinson.

One of the main features of Sutton Place today is the ancient hay meadow which runs downhill between the old chapel and the approach road. During June it is a delightful mixture of white, yellow and red with ox-eye daisies (*Chrysanthemum leucanthemum*), buttercups (*Ranunculus* spp.) and corn poppies (*Papaver rhoeas*).

Right: *Agriculturalists have done their best to rid cornfields of their colourful weeds. Now naturalists and gardeners are trying to re-establish them as ornamental flowers. Common corn poppies, cornflowers, corn marigolds and corncockles are now infrequent in their natural habitats but make stimulating displays when reintroduced as medieval meadows.*

Above: *The Paradise Garden at Sutton Place, Surrey, one of a series of delightfully varied garden "compartments" that are a feature of Sutton Place.*

In his grand plan for the gardens at Sutton Place – said to be the greatest gardening scheme since Chatsworth – Jellicoe has been particularly kind to wildlife on the estate. The newly created 10 ha (25 acre) lake in front of the house recalls the grand earth-moving schemes of Capability Brown. It already attracts mallards, tufted duck, pochard and little ringed plovers which nest on the banks, while mandarin ducks find a home among the old pollarded willows. Sir Peter Scott, the famous ornithologist, advises as a Trustee of the Sutton Place Heritage Trust. The meadows are left free to blossom each year with a startling array of wild flowers, and butterflies flutter from head to head. Snipe, duck and swans visit the wetter meadows. Old woods have been left untouched and are now managed for wildlife.

The breakdown of the gardens into smaller areas recalls the Lutyens style and his fascination with enclosing walls. The gardens are expressly designed so that the arts can be appreciated, but the house and grounds have a feel of a typical Tudor home, not a museum. The specially built Nicholson wall offers a backdrop for herbaceous borders (a Jekyll speciality), a place for espalier fruit trees and a shelter for less hardy plants. The wild garden was designed for special plants, as Robinson preferred, and even mosses are brought

THE
PARSON-NATURALISTS

It seems to be a peculiarly British characteristic that many of our keenest naturalist-gardeners have been parsons. Probably the best-known name is that of Reverend Gilbert White of Selborne, the eighteenth-century naturalist, (see page 88), though he was but one of a distinguished tradition.

Many parson-naturalists perhaps enjoyed the overgrown nature of some of the glebe lands (land belonging to the church) and churchyards. The long grass would be full of brown butterflies, beetles, crickets and grasshoppers, with meadow pipits (*Anthus pratensis*) and skylarks (*Alauda gulgula*) in the open areas. The nightingale (*Luscinia megarhynchos*) would sing from the copses. Occasional visitors to these old churchyards would have been badgers (*Meles meles*) and foxes (*Vulpes vulpes*), whilst at harvest time hedgehogs (*Erinaceus europaeus*), hares (*Lepus capensis*) and harvest mice (*Micromys minutus*) would seek refuge. No wonder that so many clergy were keen naturalists. Wild life was all around them and its beauty contrasted strongly with the poverty and disease to be found in many of their parishes.

In Britain mulberry trees (*Morus nigra*) are often found in both churchyards and vicarage gardens because many clergymen responded to James I's edict to have them planted for feeding silkworms in his grand plan to produce silk for the Huguenot refugees. Yew trees (*Taxus baccata*)

were respected for their longevity and wind-break features. Continental cemeteries and ecclesiastical gardens blossom with the Funeral Cypress (*Cupressus sempervirens*), Lombardy poplars (*Populus nigra italica*) or the tall Californian Redwoods (*Sequoia sempervirens*). Among the parson-naturalists noted for distinguished plantings was Henry Compton (1632-1713), Lord Bishop of London, who had a fine collection of trees, especially those from North America, in his grounds at Fulham and who was in touch with leading botanists of the day.

Churchyards and cemeteries were often created from flower-rich meadows and have subsequently missed the herbicides and ploughing up of adjacent fields. They are still rich in species, and remain important reservoirs for flora and fauna.

More recently, other parson-naturalists have established fine gardens or have been interested in particular groups of flowers. The Reverend Samuel Hole (1819-1904), Dean of Rochester, Kent, helped to found The National Rose Society, and the Reverend Andrew Foster-Melliar from Sproughton, Suffolk, wrote *The Book of the Rose*, a classic, which was published posthumously in 1905. The Reverend Henry Jardine Bidder (1847-1923) was the founder of rock gardening, and the Reverend Joseph H. Pemberton bred fragrant musk roses, such as *Moonlight, Penelope* and *Thisbe*.

Canon Henry Nicholson Ellacombe (1822-1916) took over his father's garden at Bitton Vicarage, near Bath. It already contained a notable plant collection, which included 250 rose varieties. Canon Ellacombe was a friend of Gertrude Jekyll and of Dean Hole, and other keen gardeners of the time, whom he often supplied with plants. He also made regular contributions to Kew. He published *Plant Lore of Shakespeare* (1875), *In a Gloucestershire Garden* (1895), and *In My Vicarage Garden and Elsewhere* (1902).

The Reverend C. Wolley Dod was another parson who created a fine garden at Edge Hall, earning special appreciation from William Robinson, Gertrude Jekyll and the alpine collector, Reginald Farrer. He frequently contributed to gardening publications such as *Gardener's Chronicle* and *The Garden*, and his name is commemorated in Wolley Dod's rose, *Rosa pomifera duplex*.

One of the most famous plants associated with a vicar is the Shirley Poppy, named after the Reverend William Wilks (1843-1923), who lived at Shirley on the outskirts of Croydon, Surrey, earlier this century. He personally selected a different colour strain from the common field poppy, which became known as the Shirley Poppy. Wilks was secretary to the Royal Horticultural Society and his poppies are commemorated on the wrought iron gates at Wisley, Surrey. Seeds of poppies were traded world wide by Wilks, who was able to boast that "gardens of the whole world, rich man's and poor man's alike, are today furnished with poppies". When Wilks retired he created a wilderness garden in the Robinson tradition, for the appreciation of colourful plants growing in abandon.

In the present century the Reverend William Keble Martin is well known for his *Concise British Flora in Colour*, which was first published in 1965. He read botany at Oxford before entering the Church and he was an enthusiastic collector who illustrated an amazing 1,486 species in his book. His meticulous paintings represent 60 years of work, fitted in with his religious responsibilities. He would travel widely throughout Britain between services and often drew many of his collected specimens whilst returning on the train. Many of the wild plants he painted are now more frequently seen in the garden. Most are very localized in the wild, though marsh marigold (*Caltha palustris*) can be spectacular and is abundant in wet woods and meadows.

The Californian Tree poppy (Romneya coulteri) was named after the Reverend Romney Robinson (1792-1882), who made a study of the plants in his garden in Armagh, Northern Ireland.

A set of wild flower stamps designed by the Reverend William Keble Martin (1877-1969). They were issued in April 1967. Keble Martin was a keen lepidopterist and botanist from an early age.

George Forrest (1873-1932).

Left: *This is a real "Flame of the Forest", since the new red leaves of* Pieris formosa forrestii *stand out in the mountains of China where George Forrest collected. On one expedition to collect plants only one of his 17 collectors and servants survived a religious massacre.*

to the forefront as a centrepiece in the moss or secret garden, ringing one of the trees – a most original feature, seen hardly anywhere else in gardens.

TWENTIETH-CENTURY NATURALISTS

Despite the revival of interest in native plants and simple cottage garden flowers, the search for new species and exotic plants did not cease at the end of the nineteenth century but has continued up to the present day. Some of the most important contributions to present-day gardens such as Great Dixter and Hidcote have been made by naturalists and botanists of the early part of the century. Frank Kingdon Ward (1885-1958), for instance, collected in China, Assam, Burma and Tibet, bringing back among other treasures the magnificent blue Himalayan poppy, *Meconopsis betonicifolia*. Ernest Henry Wilson (1876-1930) penetrated the unknown depths of China to bring out specimens of the pocket-handkerchief or dove tree (*Davidia involucrata*) and species of lily, including the splendid *Lilium regale*, and Reginald Farrer (1880-1920) specialized in alpine plants. The indefatigable Scot, George Forrest (1873-1932), facing appalling dangers in China, sent back scores of plant species which are now familiar garden plants, among them several clematis species and the lovely shrub *Pieris formosa* var. *forrestii* with its red-tipped juvenile leaves. There is a

specimen of this raised from material sent back by Forrest at Wakehurst Place, in East Sussex.

But today a key word has crept into our vocabulary – conservation; and in the second half of our century a new consciousness has grown of the need to preserve the habitats of rare plants and animals, and to make the best possible use of the knowledge that we already have. The trends towards more natural methods of garden making and cultivation of plants, a curb upon the use of herbicides and the improvement of existing species by hybridization have accelerated since the Second World War.

Much of the growing awareness of the fragility of the ecological balance began with the publication of American author Rachel Carson's *Silent Spring*, a book which painted a chilling picture of a dying world. She was more of an ecologist and conservationist than a naturalist, but she did her share of practical nature study. She bought a stretch of the Maine coast and built a cottage overlooking the tidal pools where she could study the typical marine life of the region, the seaweeds, invertebrates and seawater vertebrates. She also had a house in a wooded area at Silver Spring, Maryland, where she did much of her writing.

Not all naturalists' gardens are the inviting wildernesses that one might expect – Darwin's, for instance, was particularly clean and tidy. Some naturalists choose to live in an isolated area brimming with wildlife and therefore have no need to create a wild garden. Most of my own small garden near Battle, in East Sussex, however, is a wilderness, an unattractive jungle of plants left to their own devices. Of some concern to friendly neighbours who would prefer to garden without wind-blown weeds, it often appears like a vacant lot. But it is teeming with life.

The bees in the apiary hum over the nettles chasing comma and small tortoiseshell butterflies (*Polygonia c-album* and *Aglais urticae*), which like to bask on their hives. Attractive "weeds" always have priority in this part of the garden; perhaps a stout hogweed (*Heracleum sphondylium*), or ragwort (*Senecio jacobaea*) may actually be given some encouragement. Both Russian and tuberous comfrey (*Symphytum x uplandicum* and *S. tuberosum*) have been introduced to the garden and grow wild beside green alkanet (*Pentaglottis sempervirens*), tansy (*Chrysanthemum vulgare*) and aquilegia which were already there. In the spring the orange tip butterflies find food plants in the pretty cuckoo flower (*Arum maculatum*). Various buddleias have been planted in the garden and these attract peacocks (*Inachis io*) and red admirals (*Vanessa atalanta*) which also visit decaying windfalls later in the autumn along with speckled woods (*Pararge aegeria*). Meadow browns and gatekeepers (*Maniola jurtina* and *Pyronia tithonus*) thrive in the long grass as well as crickets and glow-worms (*Lampyris noctiluca*). My neighbour's rampant ivy-clad hedge is ideal for the holly blue butterfly (*Celastrina argiolus*), whose caterpillars feed here. There are always two generations of the butterflies in the garden. The grassy tufts are full of slow-worms (*Anguis fragilis*) and dormice inhabit the hedgerow banks, though their nests are seen more frequently than they are themselves.

This is a part of Sussex which is well wooded and consequently cuckoos and nightingales tend to be very common each year. The gardens are always invaded by magpies (*Pica pica*) and jays (*Garrulus glandarius*) which unfortunately take nesting birds' eggs, even those of the spotted flycatcher (*Muscicapa striata*) which always breeds in the open-plan nest-box. Starlings (*Sturnus vulgaris*) try to get the blue tit chicks out of their box, in which a pair of nuthatches (*Sitta europaea*) frequently nest. A peregrine falcon (*Falco peregrinus*) was seen in the garden once, having just taken one of the swallows (*Hirundo rustica*) nesting in the nearby stable.

At night my "jungle" is the favourite foraging ground for the tawny owl (*Strix aluco*) which screeches like mad searching for small mammals; by day it is the turn of the kestrel (*Falco tinnunculus*). A barn owl (*Tyto alba*) quarters the ground occasionally. I also have a resident colony of 50-odd serotine bats (*Vespertilio serotinus*) which live in the cavity walls of my cottage and forage far and wide during the spring and summer.

In this large expanse of grassy jungle I try to keep a kitchen garden which supplies some regular crops such as asparagus and raspberries.

The great problem about leaving an area to itself is that it is liable to be taken over by one or two vigorous plants

John Feltwell in his garden. Grazing sheep and scratching chickens control growth in part of the wilder area of long, lank grasses rich in butterflies, glow-worms, slow-worms and dormice.

which you do not want in vast quantity, especially stinging nettles (*Urtica* spp.) and brambles. Stern action is required to limit their advance. The form of biological control I use is muscle power – never herbicides. Most of the jungle area is selectively grazed by Celtic Soay sheep. These keep the wildlife diversity and control the rampant growth that has developed over five years.

Around the house the garden is what I call semi-formal. Here I have planted rare and interesting species, like the small-leaved lime (*Tilia cordata*), spindle (*Euonymus europaeus*), manna ash (*Fraxinus ornus*) and my favourite mulberry trees, white and black (*Morus alba* and *M. nigra*) and a new Japanese variety. I have old-fashioned pillar roses, fritillaries in the spring, gunnera, purple loosestrife (*Lythrum salicaria*) and a collection of willows (*Salix* spp.) in the wetter parts.

The hedgerows I have allowed to grow up as far as they like. In places I have laid the hedge where screening is not so important, being careful to leave sapling trees as future standards. The rampant growth has allowed bullace to flower and fruit prolifically and I look forward to its fruits each year. I encourage garlands of honeysuckle and hops which are naturalized in my 400-year-old hedge. Some of the undergrowth is full of arum lilies and lesser celandine in the spring and I have been careful to look after the spiky butcher's broom (*Ruscus aculeatus*), which is a typical woodland and hedgerow plant in this region.

I have rose beds and small lawns which I mow more for convenience and recreation than for their good looks. I certainly do not weed out the broad-leaved plants; in fact I encourage daisies, dandelions and moss. If scarlet pimpernel (*Anagallis arvensis*) pops up in the rose bed (as it does each year) I encourage it to smother the soil with its long stems 1 m (3 ft) in length. Bistort (*Polygonum bistorta*) and thorn apples (*Datura stramonium*) were surprises which came up when some soil was moved and are carefully looked after. Other interesting species, such as apple of Peru (*Nicandra physalodes*) and some of the seeds I brought back from the jungles of Sulawesi in Indonesia when collecting seed for Kew's seed bank, are grown on here experimentally.

CHAPTER EIGHT

CREATING
THE
NATURALIST'S PARADISE

Our gardens are becoming increasingly important as sanctuaries for once-common plants and animals now threatened with extinction. By planting different mini-habitats, we can attract a fascinating variety of wildlife and help to conserve many threatened species of flora and fauna.

Mixed hedges will attract all kinds of insects – and the birds and small mammals that feed upon them. A water garden will quickly become home for thousands of amphibians – if it is big enough it could attract a pair of mallards or coots. Instead of removing an old tree, leave it – a barn owl might nest there. If you don't have a hollow tree, an old tea-chest will provide an equally effective nesting site. Bats are an endangered species and you can help to establish your own bat colony buy making or buying a bat box. By creating and maintaining an imaginative diversity, we can establish truly "living" gardens that will be enjoyed by benefactors and beneficiaries alike.

Climbing roses cascade through an old apple tree in this Norfolk garden.

Naturalists dream of leafy green wild places abounding in wildlife. Their gardens are an expression of their attempts to recreate some of those exceptional habitats they have found in the wild. Like any gardener or plantsman, the naturalist likes to create different mini-habitats within a single garden, perhaps a limestone garden, a peat bed or a pond, stocked with unusual species. The plant selection of every garden depends primarily on the type of soil, but there is always room for small diversions into these mini-habitats, to beat the system and create a novel patch of foreign vegetation.

Though a few exotic or alien plants might be included as a reminder of former travels, the naturalist nearly always tries to encourage *native* species, since they harbour a greater diversity of insects than any other plants and keeping the insect numbers high will encourage other forms of wildlife. Such a garden is often left to its own devices – an area of rampant vegetation where the successful weeds are often of greater importance to wildlife than cultivated species. Subspecies and "sports" (mutations) are also encouraged; so too are rare or threatened species.

All naturalists' gardens should contain wild chrysanthemums, such as marguerites or ox-eye daisies (*Chrysanthemum leucanthemum*), or feverfew (*C. parthenium*), which has a delightful yellow-leaved form. Some plants take over gardens, set seed everywhere (sometimes upsetting neighbours) and are difficult to eradicate. Many traditional cottage garden plants such as tansy (*C. vulgare*) and columbine (*Aquilegia vulgaris*) owe their survival to this characteristic. The acanthus (*Acanthus mollis*) is another plant which sets up strong roots.

PLANTS FOR THE BORDER

Having often seen the same mixture of species growing in unchecked glory in some distant place, the keen naturalist enjoys colourful herbaceous borders, rock gardens and flower beds as much as any cottage gardener, often buying wild flower seed to supplement the selection of plants. Chemicals, however, will never be used.

The herbaceous border of an English garden is unique, a creation of the moist, unremarkably warm climate that promotes plant growth and is the envy of many plant growers in other parts of the world. At the foot of the border various native plants, such as lady's mantle (*Alchemilla mollis*) and

a host of geraniums like the oak-leaved or the blazing bloody cranesbill, *Geranium sanguineum* – its flowers stunning in their quantity – are plants typical of rocky mountainous slopes. Saxifrages, or "rock-splitters" from their Latin and anglicized name, are now firm favourites and do well on well-drained soils, particularly in rock gardens. I have seen mountain avens (*Dryas octopetala*) growing better in ordinary gardens (as is frequently the case) than in the wild, where clumps adorn barren limestone areas as far as the cyc can see, and the fluffy fruits are still visible five months later. Gentians, a favourite amongst enthusiasts, are reminders of alpine pastures and heathy wastes. St Patrick's cabbage (*Saxifraga spathularis*), that Irish plant found also in Spain and Portugal which hugs the leafy hillsides, is similar to the more familiar London Pride (another saxifrage), and deserves a place in any garden. So, too, do the delicate purple flowers of the woodland hepatica (*Hepatica nobilis*), or the elusive herb paris (*Paris quadrifolia*) with its striking black fruit, rarely seen in gardens.

Colourful plants to supplement spring bulbs are the winter-flowering pansies, forget-me-not (*Myosotis* spp.), bugle (*Ajuga* spp. – there are some interesting dark-leaved forms) and marsh marigold (*Caltha palustris*) if you have wet land; there is a beautiful double variety. Lilies (especially the Mediterranean Martagon lily), tulips and muscari offer splashes of colour and enormous variety in the early borders. Native orchids can be integrated into the garden, whether woody species, such as the early purple (*Orchis mascula*), or delicately flowered and rare species, like lady's slipper (*Cypripedium calceolus*). Through the early part of the year the garden can be enlivened with the scented purple flowers of mezereon, *Daphne mezereum* (there is also an albino variety), and its relation from the woods, spurge laurel (*Daphne laureola*). The exquisite green bell-like flowers of the latter can often be seen flowering in the snow.

Later on in the summer campanulas, salvias, poppies and loosestrifes (*Lythrum* spp.) provide a magnificent array of colours. There are tall campanulas, tiny ones and those that cavort over walls as well. My favourite salvia is *pratensis* or meadow clary, an adulteration of "clear eye", since the seeds were used to clean the eyes. The most spectacular loosestrife is the purple one (*Lythrum salicaria*), much more useful as a food plant for wildlife than the more frequently planted yellow species (*Lysimachia vulgaris*). There seems to be no end to the choice of poppies which you can buy as annuals, Welsh (*Meconopsis cambrica*), Californian (*Eschscholzia*)

Above: With tiny leaves the shape of miniature oak leaves, the mountain avens (Dryas octopetala) *enjoys moist and rugged habitats. Its white flowers contrast with the nodding yellow heads of the Welsh poppy (*Meconopsis cambrica, left*). Many other species of meconopsis have blue flowers.*

or opium (*Papaver somniferum*); they are all pretty. Naturalists often prefer the delicate garden pinks, such as the Cheddar pink (*Dianthus gratianopolitanus*), rather than the much larger dianthus, the traditional Sweet Williams of cottage gardens. Herbs in the garden are always welcome, whether they be Russian comfrey (*Symphytum x uplandicum*), known as the compost plant because it is so mineral-rich, whose leaves can be steeped in water in an old bath to provide a liquid plant tonic, or banks of sweet-smelling thyme, silver-leaved sage or straggly rosemary.

Hollyhocks, angelica, Scotch thistles and globe artichokes are impressively tall plants for the back of the herbaceous border, but my pride of place goes to the tree mallow (*Lavatera arborea*) which showers out sprays of blossom in all directions, and flowers for about four months, sometimes surviving the winter. Some of the hardy fuchsias (red and white ones) make excellent hedges, over a metre (3 ft) tall, typical of the warm west coast of Ireland. Other shrubs at the back of the border may include laburnum with its fine cascades of flowers, magnolias (especially *Magnolia stellata*), the woody abutilon and viburnums. But the finest is perhaps the whitebeam (*Sorbus aria*), looking at the first flush of leaves as though chalk has penetrated its distinctly white leaves.

Left: One of the finest oakwoods in England is Wistman's Wood in Devon where the gnarled oaks are surrounded by flowering plants and ferns. A wild plant of calcareous soils is the bloody cranesbill (*Geranium sanguineum, above*), which can produce some spectacular displays.

ENCOURAGING
WILD FLOWERS

With the growing concern over the loss of wild flower species from the countryside, there has been a wild flower seed boom in the 1980s as ordinary people (not necessarily just naturalists) try to re-create some of the former colours of the wild woods and meadows in their gardens.

Botanic gardens, too, have been quick to draw attention to rare plants and the reasons why they should be conserved. In England, at Cambridge Botanic Garden, rare habitats such as the Fens are re-created and planted with appropriate water-loving plants, such as marsh woundwort (*Stachys palustris*) and fen violet (*Viola stagnina*). In the States, Illinois Botanic Garden, like Kew Gardens, receives seeds from collectors in distant countries to be placed in their seed banks for research purposes. In 1985, the author collected seed for Kew from the tropical rainforests of Sulawesi in Indonesia. Much of the seed conserved in the seed banks, particularly that of members of the grass and legume families, is used in research for new crop characteristics, or in the case of euphorbias, for alternative sources of petrochemicals. Some of the species collected may turn out to be rare and eventually be grown in gardens; in any case the genetic diversity of the plants has been preserved for all time.

A favourite pastime of amateur naturalists is to establish an ancient meadow in the garden and one of the "oldest" seed mixtures available is the Cricklade Mixture. This contains 35 wild flower seeds harvested directly from an ancient meadow which lies on the banks of the upper River Thames at Cricklade in Wiltshire, part of a

*It is always challenging to grow the once common plants of the countryside such as the familiar ragged robin (*Lychnis flos-cuculi, bottom right*), sadly lost in former wetter areas, or the corn poppy (*Papaver rhoeas, bottom left*) itself an abundant plant on freshly turned soil. More infrequent but equally worth conserving is the delicate water violet (*Hottonia palustris, above*) which can smother shady pools.*

National Nature Reserve. Documentary evidence proves that this meadow has remained unploughed and untreated with chemicals for more than 800 years and it is therefore the finest remaining example of a traditional lowland meadow in Britain. No wonder everyone aspires to re-create this little bit of England in the wilder parts of their grounds. Naturalist Don MacIntyre of Emorsgate Seeds gathers seeds from this meadow every July and sends them out to gardens and farms all over Britain, Europe and America.

Habitat creation is the aim of many amateur and professional naturalists. Seed merchants have mixtures ideal for all sorts of soils: short and tall meadow mixtures for clay, calcareous and alluvial soils; special mixtures for wetland areas; and, a very popular collection, a cornfield mixture. This is bright with species such as corncockle (*Agrostemma githago*), cornflower (*Centaurea cyanus*), corn poppy (*Papaver rhoeas*), scarlet pimpernel (*Anagallis*

arvensis) and violets. Hedgerow and woodland mixtures help to reintroduce some plant species into gardens which have become infrequent in recent years, like bedstraws (*Galium* spp.), geraniums, campions and ragged robin (*Lychnis flos-cuculi*), with commoner species such as bluebells (*Endymion non-scriptus*), stitchworts and various grasses.

If you wish to establish a wild-flower meadow the first job is to find out, with the aid of a simple soil-testing kit, what type of soil you have – whether it is acidic, neutral or alkaline. This is known as its pH: the unit of measurement of hydrogen ions in the soil water.

Next, prepare the ground well and remove persistent weeds. You may have to wait several months in order to seed at the correct time. Timing will depend on the type of soil you have and the kind of meadow you want. The pH reading will indicate which seed mixture to order. Any soil can be used for growing wild flowers: it does not have to be especially fertile. Infertile soils actually have a greater rate of seed germination than fertile ones!

The next step is to sow the seed, either broadcasting by hand in a traditional manner or with a seed riddle. Different systems of management are required for each sort of meadow, but you can produce colourful flower-filled meadows by the first year. Some soils will give vigorous growth suitable for hay-making, others a short grass sward simply to be admired. Grazing is recommended during the winter months and special care over the second and third years is recommended to establish firmly a good display of wild flowers.

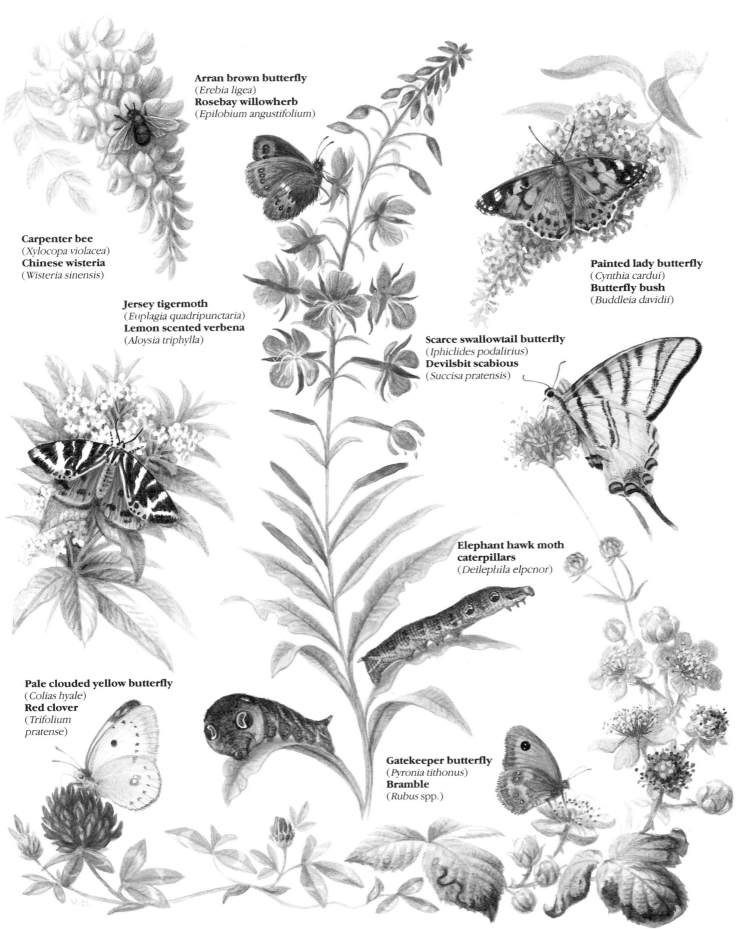

Arran brown butterfly
(*Erebia ligea*)
Rosebay willowherb
(*Epilobium angustifolium*)

Carpenter bee
(*Xylocopa violacea*)
Chinese wisteria
(*Wisteria sinensis*)

Jersey tigermoth
(*Euplagia quadripunctaria*)
Lemon scented verbena
(*Aloysia triphylla*)

Painted lady butterfly
(*Cynthia cardui*)
Butterfly bush
(*Buddleia davidii*)

Scarce swallowtail butterfly
(*Iphiclides podalirius*)
Devilsbit scabious
(*Succisa pratensis*)

**Elephant hawk moth
caterpillars**
(*Deilephila elpenor*)

Pale clouded yellow butterfly
(*Colias hyale*)
Red clover
(*Trifolium
pratense*)

Gatekeeper butterfly
(*Pyronia tithonus*)
Bramble
(*Rubus* spp.)

POISONOUS PLANTS

Several colourful border plants are poisonous if eaten raw, but medicinally important when their active constituents are extracted. The best example is foxglove (*Digitalis purpurea*) which looks good in many shady places and along hedgerows. It's a tall biennial like its frequent neighbour in the flower bed, mullein (*Verbascum* spp.). Monkshood (*Aconitum* spp.) with its attractive blue flowers and cut leaves belies its poisons, once used to tip poison darts and lace innocuous-looking drinks. Poisonous peonies flourish with gay abandon for a short while, and die back until next year; they have become naturalized in only a few places. Spurges, or euphorbias, are notoriously poisonous with their tell-tale white latex which drips from cut surfaces. But plants like the stout Mediterranean *Euphorbia characias* and its close relation *wulfenii* make splendid displays in the herbaceous border. There are plenty of other spurges for the garden, whether for shade, like wood spurge, or for the open, like sun and cypress spurges. Pretty spurge and black spurge may occur as opportunist weeds, anyway.

Other poisonous plants are the thorn apple, *Datura stramonium*, which was originally brought over from America as a medicinal plant to relieve congestion in the nasal passages, shoo-fly plants (*Nicandra* spp.) and henbane (*Hyoscyamus niger*), a European native still found growing in quantity around old towns and ruins in southern Europe. Another is the deadly nightshade (*Atropa belladona*). Many of these poisonous plants are magnificent when fully grown; but they should always be planted well out of the way of children.

WALLS AND ROOFS

Walls make excellent places to introduce many wild plants and ferns. Red valerian (*Centranthus ruber*) is superb when established. The tiny sedums which creep over the rocks, flowering infrequently, and the polypody fern, hard fern and spleenwort do well in humid environments. Houseleeks (*Sempervivum* spp.) are a must on top of sheds, roofs and walls in true William Robinson or Christopher Lloyd style.

Above: *Of exceptional importance for the herbaceous border is the attractive* Euphorbia wulfenii. *Like other members of the spurge family it is a poisonous plant.*

Left: *Tiny fragments of the wall rue (*Asplenium ruta-muraria*) are sold spuriously as shamrocks in Ireland, for it is an abundant fern of old walls. Its hard, dark green fronds are rooted in plaster and cracks in the masonry.*

The navelwort (*Umbilicus rupestris*) is a favourite of mine, seen all too infrequently on the walls of gardens. The royal fern (*Osmunda regalis*) is large and very impressive in the autumn with its orange fronds and is ideal at the base of walls or in damp woods, perhaps rubbing shoulders with butcher's broom (*Ruscus aculeatus*), those clumps of evergreen spiky stems, reputedly used for cleaning meat from the chopping block.

Climbers are often encouraged in the naturalist's garden. Morning glory is an attractive convolvulus while honeysuckle, hops and ivy are welcome additions to any hedgerow. Wisteria and Virginia creepers are popular too, especially the species with five fingers to its leaf, (*Parthenocissus quinquefolia*). But nothing can beat the rambling and climbing roses which smother a typically English cottage garden.

ENCOURAGING INSECTS

Many insects are beneficial as well as ornamental, and all provide food for amphibians, reptiles, birds and mammals. If you want to attract other forms of wildlife into the garden it is as well to encourage the insects, few of which are pests.

Insects are the most successful animals on earth and the most numerous in the garden. Every fourth animal on earth is a beetle. Thousands of insects will be in the garden already, but you can encourage more by creating different habitats for them. Many fly at night and colonize new areas very quickly.

Insects are classified into 28 different groups, technically called orders, and most of these groups are represented in the garden. They are all identified by different shapes and structures; beetles, for instance, have a hardened pair of wing cases (the elytra), butterflies and moths have scaly wings, dragonflies and damselflies have long, often transparent wings and long bodies, true flies have the second pair of wings modified into a tiny "lollipop" used aerodynamically, earwigs have pincers on the end of their abdomen, and bees, wasps and ants have a constriction between the thorax and abdomen and many of them sting.

Leaving piles of old logs is a favourite way of encouraging insects. Many like the damp conditions provided by rotting wood, especially behind peeling bark. By encouraging insects you are actually encouraging many non-insects, too; anthropods such as woodlice – (terrestrial crustaceans), as well as spiders, mites, pseudoscorpions, and harvestmen – all members of the class arachnida.

In drier parts of the log pile butterflies from the nymphalidae family (for example the small tortoiseshell, *Aglais urticae*, the large tortoiseshell, *Nymphalis polychloros*, the Camberwell beauty, *N. antiopa* and the comma *Polygonia c-album*) may hibernate in Europe. A wood shed or other outbuilding which has easy access points for butterflies

*Forgotten fruits attract the red-tinted hornet (*Vespa crabro, *above*), which may share this feast with butterflies and bees. Bumblebees, such as* Bombus pratorum, *(left) are beneficial insects and may make their small nests under sheds or in a bank.*

will also provide alternative winter quarters for hibernating insects. Scores of ladybirds may also take up their winter quarters in the wood pile or in old wooden posts, jammed together in small cracks in the wood. Earwigs, wood-boring beetles and their larvae, millipedes, centipedes and numerous spring-tails – tiny 0.07in (2mm) long primitive wingless insects which leap out of danger – may also be found, a similar collection to that found in the leafy parts of the compost heap and in the leaf litter under the hedge. Slugs and snails abound in damp places, and will be found underneath hedges or in long grass. If a plank of wood is left on the ground all sorts of wildlife will assemble there: slugs, snails, ants and even slow worms (legless lizards).

CREATING INSECT HABITATS

Bumble bees
(*Bombus lucorum*)
Cow parsley
(*Anthriscus sylvestris*)

Six-spot burnet moths
(*Zygaena filipendulae*)
Spear thistle
(*Cirsium vulgare*)

Habitats worth creating are areas of long grass or scrub, a hedgerow and a pond. Grassy orchards or gardens left to develop their own jungle-like vegetation are ideal places which butterflies, moths, flies, shield bugs and beetles will automatically colonize. The tiny skipper butterflies and a few members of the brown family of butterflies will lay their eggs on the long grasses and soon develop thriving colonies.

If you go out at night you may well find scores of different moth caterpillars. Adults of the ghost swift moth (*Hepialus humuli*) fly eerily over the grass at twilight. If willow-herb (*Epilobium* spp.) is plentiful, the caterpillars of the elephant hawk-moth may thrive; other hawk-moths can be encouraged with the introduction of willows, poplar and lime. Willows are always worth planting since they grow fast and are a staple food plant for scores of different moths. Long grass always attracts the chirping crickets – an added bonus during the summer and autumn when their songs can be heard late into the evening.

HEDGEROW INSECTS

You may be lucky enough to have a hedge-row in the garden already, but if not, one can be established in three or four years. The best plants to use are native species which attract wildlife and always grow better than intro-duced ones like some of the fast-growing conifers – Leyland cypress (*Cupressocyparis leylandii*), for instance, provides a poor habitat. Always use a variety of plants to form the hedgerow and leave the leaf litter which develops underneath untouched. It will harbour all sorts of tiny creatures from pseudoscorpions to minute beetles, all of which can be studied under a hand lens or small microscope.

There are special packets of wild flower seed specially formulated to sow in the shade of a hedge. You may like to do this to increase the plant diversity (and therefore the insect diversity) of an existing hedgerow, although some of the commoner hedgerow plants may become defoliated by the caterpillars of moths or sawflies. Their silken webs are used as a safety shield against bird predators.

Oak bush cricket
(*Meconema thalassinum*)
Teasel
(*Dipsacus fullonum*)

Green shield bugs
(*Palomena prasina*)
Wild carrot
(*Daucus carota*)

Garden snails
(*Helix aspersa*)

Above: *Common arrowhead* (Sagittaria sagittifolia) *is a very distinctive pond plant.*

Left: *Ponds can be a very attractive garden feature – and attract a multitude of fascinating creatures.*

Great diving beetle
(*Dytiscus marginalis*)

POND INSECTS

Bringing water into the garden increases the diversity of insects almost overnight. Water beetles find new water sources by flying around at night and you will soon see them in the pond. The larger ones are fierce carnivores and will eat small fish – they will even give you a nip.

There are several considerations in making a wildlife pond. First prepare the soil, removing any sharp stones. Be sure to purchase the correct type of rubber liner (the best to use is generally the most expensive one) unless you are buying a solid pre-moulded base. Plenty of water plants are essential; they not only give off vital oxygen underwater for the rest of the wildlife, but also provide good cover for invertebrates and fish fry as protection against predators. Herons can be a problem in both town and country and the best defence is to provide steep sides to the pool.

The prettiest insects to arrive by their own powers of dispersal are the powerful carnivores of the air – dragonflies, and their less powerful but equally carnivorous relatives, the damselflies. They lay their eggs underwater on vegetation and the nymphs take a few years to develop. Like their parents, the nymphs are also carnivorous and catch small insects with their extendable "masks". To have strong colonies of dragon-flies and damselflies it is essential to have plenty of vegetation under the water for shelter, and stems emerging from it for the nymphs to climb up when they are hatching. Even tiny ponds can soon attract several species. In an urban environment your pond may quickly become home to thousands of amphibians.

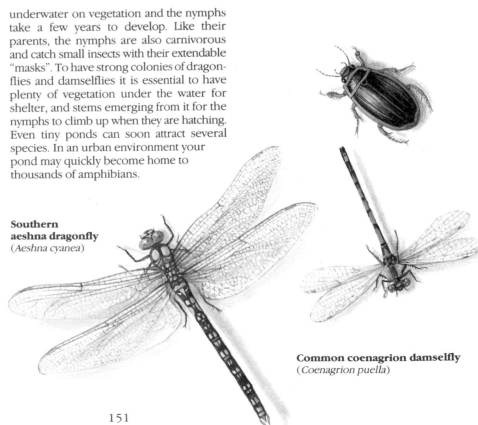

Southern aeshna dragonfly
(*Aeshna cyanea*)

Common coenagrion damselfly
(*Coenagrion puella*)

MAMMALS IN THE GARDEN

Many of the mammals which frequent the garden are nocturnal and you may not be aware that they are there. Some will be residents, whilst others will only be visitors, coming into your garden under cover of darkness. There are plenty of ways to encourage visitors – you may be practising some of them already.

If you live near forestry plantations or deciduous woodland you may not actually welcome the nocturnal visits of deer who have a discerning appetite for roses. Only a 2 m (6 ft) high fence will keep them out. The North American grey squirrel, unaffectionately known as the "tree rat" (*Neosciurus carolinensis*), now introduced into Britain, is also a frequent visitor to the garden, foraging for nuts.

Badgers (*Meles meles*) are familiar creatures, plodding along regular paths used by their forebears for centuries. They walk along these paths in only one direction, since their walks radiate out from their setts. The slide down one bank and claw marks up the other can be seen wherever their path crosses a road or lane. They nudge up fencing simply to continue along their habitual paths, while looking for invertebrates to eat. They are the gardener's friend, since they eat slugs, snails and earwigs as well as earthworms. Many badgers have become urbanized where their setts have become isolated close to house developments, often finding friendly people who feed them regularly – affectionately called "feeders". A good diet means a greater chance of survival amongst badgers.

Foxes (*Vulpes vulpes*) have become urbanized too. They moved in very quickly to the urban and industrial enviroment and have now reached plague proportions in some cities. They are more of an opportunist scavenger than badgers and originally used the network of railways to penetrate deep into the hearts of cities. Like badgers, they breed on railway embankments, in the rubble of derelict buildings, even in vacant cellars, and scavenge on refuse, particularly from private dustbins. There are also fox feeders as, indeed, there are cat feeders who maintain a high incidence of feral cats, some of which may cause a nuisance in your garden. In North America similar scavengers which venture into gardens or under houses are striped skunks (*Mephitis mephitis*), raccoons (*Procyon lotor*) and prairie dogs (*Cynomys ludovicianus*).

BIRD RESIDENTS AND VISITORS

You can always increase the chances of seeing a rare bird in your garden by supplying good nesting sites. You can buy, or build from plans, a variety of bird boxes for tits, blackbirds, flycatchers, owls and kestrels. Provided they are erected in the best possible place, the chances of them being used is very high. Tits will frequently use boxes the day they are put up. Remember to face them northwards so the chicks will not roast in the sun, and remember to empty the old nest out, to encourage another brood.

Above: *Urbanized badgers are now common and wily to the ways of man, especially where they are encouraged by "feeders" – people who feed them.*

Right: *Harvest mice* (Micromys minutus) *frequent roadside verges, abandoned factory sites and overgrown gardens, but are not as common in wild gardens as dormice. They construct a ball-shaped nest in long grass.*

Above: Using the beams provided by man to support their nests, swallows (Hirundo rustica) find plenty of breeding places in old barns and stables. The young grow their majestic tails after they have left the nest.

The simplest bird box of all is for the barn owl (*Tyto alba*), a threatened species in Britain. All that is required is an old tea-chest lightly filled with hay bedding material, and supported horizontally on a beam. It has to be set up in an old barn or similar building, even a church tower, with a suitable flight hole through which the birds can come and go. Hollow trees are ideal for roosting owls, but they have become so rare in the agricultural countryside that their absence has contributed to the demise of owls as well as bats. If you have an old tree in your garden, keep it.

Swallows (*Hirundo rustica*) can be encouraged to nest on beams in open-access barns, stables and other buildings, and house martins (*Delichon urbica*) will take readily to artificial nests set up under the eaves. A damp area of garden, or track with puddles, is likely to be used by house martins for collecting mud used in their nest construction. Swifts (*Apus apus*) may already be nesting under the tiles of your roof, especially in southern Europe, or in a barn, but they too can be encouraged to visit a swift box suspended underneath a bridge or arch with a flight hole on the underside. Of quite recent design, these have not yet been widely used in gardens.

The scavenging black-headed gull (*Larus ridibundus*) often frequents urban gardens. Its success is due to its exploitation of man's rubbish and it is partial to raiding bird tables. Even the kestrel (*Falco tinnunculus*) has changed its diet and has been seen to take small birds in London's gardens.

The herring gull (*Larus argentatus*) has been a nuisance, breeding on the flat-topped pebble dash rooftops (they are

Above: Mallards (Anas platyrhynchos) *frequently visit larger ponds and may even breed there. Males have the distinctive green head and maroon breast; the females are a discreet brown colour with a blue flash on the wing.*

Left: *Feral pigeons (Columba sp.) of city centres like Trafalgar Square are descended from wild rock doves but can be identified by the two dark bars across the wings.*

ENCOURAGING SMALL MAMMALS <u>AND</u> BIRDS

Living perhaps unnoticed in your attic you may have a colony of bats. These gregarious mammals come and go with the bare minimum of sound; they are creatures which fly off after sundown and return before dawn. They are beneficial since they eat a vast array of flying insects, many of them pests of garden plants. In Britain all bats are now protected and any interference with colonies in the roof or cavity walls is strictly an offence.

The commonest species to live in the attic is the pipistrelle bat (*Pipistrellus pipistrellus*), a tiny species which could exist as a colony of 80, all crammed into a small area – they only need a gap in the woodwork of 3 cm to gain access to the roof space. What the countryside lacks in the form of natural habitats for bats (such as caves) is amply made up by the artificial attic caves and cavity walls of houses – provided they can gain access. Personally, I like my own resident serotine bats (*Vespertilio serotinus*); they, like all bats, have disease-free droppings which aid in cavity-wall insulation!

Special lean-to shelters can be made to encourage hedgehogs in the garden and there is considerable enjoyment in seeing a family feeding at a saucer of bread and milk. Hedgehogs may hibernate at the base of shrubs where autumn leaves have piled up.

If you want some bats but haven't got any, then you can make or buy a bat box. These should always be situated high off the ground (higher than a garage) and face south, so that the young can benefit from the warmth of the sun. This is the opposite direction to bird boxes.

MICE, MOLES AND HEDGEHOGS

A host of small mammals such as mice, shrews and voles will find the areas of long grass in an orchard or flower meadow much to their liking. To keep out of sight of predatory birds they make runs beneath mats of old grass. You can encourage more small mammals by laying sheets of corrugated iron or wood across the ground. Small mammals will continue their runs beneath this safe haven and may even construct a grass nest beneath it. From time to time you can lift the sheet up carefully and see the variety of wildlife there – perhaps a bumble

Right: *Noctule bats* (Nyctalus noctula) *may breed in roof spaces during the summer, but they may be disturbed by starlings, especially in their other sites such as hollow trees in parks. They have a large wingspan and can often be seen flying before dusk in company with swallows and martins, catching insects in flight often close to the ground.*

bee's nest, black ground beetles, a shrew with its typical elongated nose or a mouse or a vole with its blunt head.

Dormice are innocuous small mammals that you may have in your hedgerow or long grass without knowing it. You may see the tell-tale balls of grass or honeysuckle bark, finely shredded, in which they have their young or hibernate through the winter.

The mole (*Talpa europaea*) causes consternation when it throws up its hills in the tidy lawn, but it minds its own business, trundling along its network of tunnels which are designed as a trap into which invertebrates, many of them garden pests, fall.

A scavenger in the long grass and thickets is the hedgehog (*Erinaceus europaeus*), whose nocturnal wanderings may take it into a dozen gardens or so. In some urban areas feeders put out bread and milk to encourage them, but they find enough food during the summer with beetles, caterpillars, earthworms, slugs, millipedes and earwigs to feed on. A makeshift lean-to of wood put up against a garden shed or fence and filled

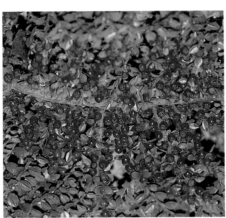

*Autumn fruits of garden plants such as cotoneaster (above), pyracantha, hawthorn or ivy make good pickings for birds like the blackbird (*Turdus merula, below), especially during cold weather.*

with straw is an ideal way of encouraging hedgehogs into the garden. They may even stay to hibernate in the construction you have made.

PLANTS TO ENCOURAGE BIRDS

Naturalist's gardens should always be filled with native trees and shrubs since the number of insect species becomes high, and this attracts insect-feeding birds. Trees such as oak, lime, alder, willow and hazel provide valuable food; clumps and thickets of bramble offer good nesting sites. Caterpillars of smaller moths support the summer populations of tits (*Parus* spp.), which decline sharply in the autumn if other food sources are not available. Spring and summer visitors like the cuckoo, flycatchers, nuthatches and warblers need a rich supply of insects while they fledge and the denser the vegetation the better.

Autumn feasts for birds could be provided with a variety of plants such as the guelder rose, (*Viburnum opulus*), cotoneasters, privet (*Ligustrum vulgare*), honeysuckle (*Lonicera* spp.) and ivy (*Hedera helix*). Goldfinches always like the old heads of teasel (*Dipsacus* spp.) from which to extract seeds, and lawns provide ample space where the green woodpecker can extract ants and other delicacies. Hollow old trees and artificial nestboxes will often encourage woodpeckers to nest.

In the hedgerow hips, haws and holly berries attract migratory redwings (*Turdus iliacus*) and fieldfares (*Turdus pilaris*) which fly into western Europe and Britain from central Europe and Russia each winter. Occasionally flocks of waxwings (*Bombycilla garrulus*) descend into gardens to feast on the berries of many plants, including rowans and juniper. Robins, dunnocks (*Prunella modularis*) and tiny wrens like thick undergrowth and leaf litter to have a good scratch around for small invertebrates, and the song thrush, too, enjoys snails it finds there.

rather similar to shingle beaches) of seaside towns for decades, and venturing to parks and gardens for food. Other rooftop roosters, such as the redshank (*Tringa totanus*) and oyster catchers (*Haematopus ostralegus*), keep out of the garden.

So the quarrelsome starlings (*Sturnus vulgaris*) have had some heavy competition from gulls in the garden, though they are still successful in this environment for feeding, breeding and roosting. Sparrows and finches are regular visitors to the bird table too. An area of rough vegetation, or mossy bank, is likely to induce the wren (*Troglodytes troglodytes*) to stay around and search for small insect prey. It is the commonest bird in Britain, but it is not frequently seen around the house. Predators which visit the garden from time to time are the magpie (*Pica pica*) and the jay (*Garrulus glandarius*), taking many fledglings and eggs from their nests.

A pond is always likely to encourage a pair of mallards (*Anas platyrhynchos*) to visit and breed there, and even a pair of moorhens (*Gallinula chloropus*) or coot (*Fulica atra*) if there is plenty of overhanging vegetation and thickets. A duck box could be erected in mid-winter.

If you have a big, rambling house in the country, you may be lucky enough to have a kestrel roosting on the side of the house, just as they do on ledges of high-rise buildings. The birds hunt over the garden for small mammals from time to time. Pairs of collared doves (*Streptopelia decaocto*) will occasionally nest on buildings, but prefer trees. Since the

1930s they have swept westwards across Europe and are now a familiar species in Britain that few fail to see. They have moved into some habitats where the resident wood-pigeon (*Columba palumbus*) used to be, but they do overlap in places.

The abundant pigeon of city centres and gardens, as in London, is the feral pigeon or stock dove (*Columba oenas*), descended from the now rare rock dove. In parts of the London suburbs, especially in parks and gardens, the escaped rose-ringed parakeet (*Psittacula krameri*) is now living feral in some substantial flocks which have been able to withstand hard winters.

In southern Europe the white stork (*Ciconia ciconia*) may nest on chimneys overlooking gardens, but it feeds in wetland lagoons far away.

Left and below: All forms of wildlife have an uncanny ability to colonize man-made habitats, seabirds nesting in coastal towns or docks, and the mute swan (Cygnus olor) becoming plentiful in towns and cities through "the bread factor" – people feeding swans from bridges. In the wild, mute swans fare less well.

Right: Azalea, "the king of shrubs", in full flower.

Birds, mammals, insects and plants are the interrelated components of the natural world, and a garden is a microcosm of this teeming life around us. Most house owners enjoy a well-ordered garden, stocked with decorative plants and all the amenities that accompany a modern life-style. But the rewards of creating a naturalist's paradise are also immense, as many people are beginning to discover. Not only is there endless interest to be gained from the wide assortment of wildlife that takes up residence there, but you will also have the satisfaction of knowing that you are providing a home for many endangered species in a world where natural habitats are being despoiled at an alarming rate.

Through the centuries, at each stage of civilization, there have been men who were close to nature and concerned with the natural world about them, whose scientific curiosity and love of beauty have taken them a step further towards enlightenment. We are all part of the life-cycle and inter-dependence of species in this world. Let us hope that, acting in ignorance and greed, we do not destroy it.

INDEX